United States Government Accountability Office

Report to the Committee on Science, Space, and Technology, House of Representatives

I0448638

September 2013

POLAR WEATHER SATELLITES

NOAA Identified Ways to Mitigate Data Gaps, but Contingency Plans and Schedules Require Further Attention

GAO Highlights

Highlights of GAO-13-676, a report to the Committee on Science, Space, and Technology, House of Representatives

POLAR WEATHER SATELLITES

NOAA Identified Ways to Mitigate Data Gaps, but Contingency Plans and Schedules Require Further Attention

Why GAO Did This Study

NOAA established the JPSS program in 2010 to replace aging polar satellites and provide critical environmental data used in forecasting weather and measuring variations in climate. However, program officials anticipate a gap in satellite data between the time that the S-NPP satellite reaches the end of its life and the JPSS-1 satellite becomes operational (see graphic). Given the criticality of satellite data to weather forecasts, the likelihood of a significant satellite data gap, and the potential impact of a gap on the health and safety of the U.S. population and economy, GAO added this issue to its High Risk List in 2013.

GAO was asked to review the JPSS program because of the importance of polar satellite data. GAO's objectives were to (1) evaluate NOAA's progress in sustaining the continuity of NOAA's polar-orbiting satellite system through S-NPP and JPSS satellites; (2) evaluate the quality of NOAA's program schedule; and (3) assess NOAA's plans to address potential gaps in polar satellite data. To do so, GAO analyzed program management status reports, milestone reviews, and schedule data; examined polar gap contingency plans; and interviewed agency and contractor officials.

What GAO Recommends

GAO is recommending NOAA develop a mechanism to track the usage of its satellite products, establish a complete integrated master schedule, address weaknesses in component schedules, and address shortfalls in polar satellite gap contingency plans. NOAA concurred with GAO's recommendations and identified steps it is taking to implement them.

View GAO-13-676. For more information, contact Dave Powner at (202) 512-9286 or pownerd@gao.gov.

What GAO Found

The National Oceanic and Atmospheric Administration (NOAA) has made noteworthy progress on the Joint Polar Satellite System (JPSS) program by delivering data from its first satellite—the Suomi National Polar-orbiting Partnership (S-NPP)—to weather forecasters, completing significant instrument development for the next satellite (called JPSS-1), and reducing the program's life cycle cost estimate from $12.9 billion to $11.3 billion by refocusing on weather products. However, key challenges remain. Specifically, S-NPP has not yet achieved full operational capability because the program is behind schedule in validating the readiness of satellite products. Also, the program does not track whether key users are using its products or if the products meet the users' needs. In addition, issues with the JPSS ground system schedules have delayed the delivery of key system capabilities. Until the program addresses these challenges, it may continue to experience delays in delivering actionable S-NPP data to system users and in meeting JPSS-1 development schedules.

A program's success depends in part on having an integrated master schedule that defines when and how long work will occur and how activities are related to each other; however, the JPSS program office does not yet have a complete integrated master schedule and weaknesses exist in component schedules. Specifically, the program established an integrated master schedule in June 2013 and is reporting a 70 percent confidence level in the JPSS-1 launch date. However, about one-third of the program schedule is missing information needed to establish the sequence in which activities occur. In addition, selected component schedules supporting the JPSS-1 satellite have weaknesses including schedule constraints that have not been justified. Until the program completes its integrated schedule and addresses weaknesses in component schedules, it will lack the information needed to effectively monitor development progress and have less assurance of meeting the planned JPSS-1 launch date.

While NOAA developed a mitigation plan to address a potential 14 to 18 month gap in afternoon polar satellite data in October 2012 and subsequently identified additional alternatives for addressing potential gaps, it has not yet established a comprehensive contingency plan. Specifically, NOAA has not yet revised its mitigation plan to include the new alternatives, and the plan lacks several key elements, such as triggers for when to take key actions and detailed procedures for implementing them. Until NOAA establishes a comprehensive plan, it may not be sufficiently prepared to mitigate anticipated gaps in polar satellite coverage.

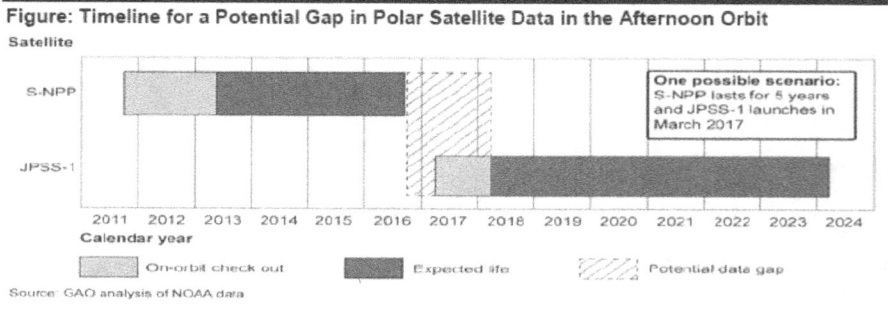

Figure: Timeline for a Potential Gap in Polar Satellite Data in the Afternoon Orbit

Source: GAO analysis of NOAA data.

_____ United States Government Accountability Office

Contents

Figures

Abbreviations

A-DCS	Advanced Data Collection System
ATMS	Advanced Technology Microwave Sounder
CERES	Cloud and Earth's Radiant Energy System
CrIS	Cross-Track Infrared Sounder
DMSP	Defense Meteorological Satellite Program
DOD	Department of Defense
IDPS	Interface Data Processing Segment
JCL	Joint Cost and Schedule Confidence Level
JPSS	Joint Polar Satellite System
MetOp	Meteorological Operational (satellite)
NASA	National Aeronautics and Space Administration
NESDIS	National Environmental Satellite, Data, and Information Service
NOAA	National Oceanic and Atmospheric Administration
NPOESS	National Polar-orbiting Operational Environmental Satellite System
S-NPP	Suomi National Polar-orbiting Partnership
OMPS	Ozone Mapping and Profiler Suite
POES	Polar-orbiting Operational Environmental Satellites
TSIS	Total and Spectral Solar Irradiance Sensor
VIIRS	Visible/Infrared Imager/Radiometer Suite

September 11, 2013

The Honorable Lamar Smith
Chairman
The Honorable Ralph Hall
Chairman Emeritus
The Honorable Eddie Bernice Johnson
Ranking Member
Committee on Science, Space, and Technology
House of Representatives

The National Polar-orbiting Operational Environmental Satellite System (NPOESS) program was planned to be a state-of-the-art, environment-monitoring satellite system that would replace two existing polar-orbiting environmental satellite systems. Managed jointly by the Department of Commerce's National Oceanic and Atmospheric Administration (NOAA), the Department of Defense (DOD)/U.S. Air Force, and the National Aeronautics and Space Administration (NASA), the program was considered critical to the nation's ability to maintain the continuity of data required for weather forecasting and global climate monitoring through the year 2026.

However, in the 8 years after the development contract was awarded in 2002, the NPOESS cost estimate had more than doubled—to about $15 billion, launch dates had been delayed by over 5 years, significant functionality had been removed from the program, and the program's tri-agency management structure had proven to be ineffective. Importantly, delays in launching the satellites put the program's mission at risk. To address these challenges, a task force led by the White House's Office of Science and Technology Policy reviewed the management and governance of the NPOESS program. In February 2010, the Director of the Office of Science and Technology Policy announced a decision to disband the NPOESS acquisition and, instead, have NOAA and DOD undertake separate acquisitions, with NOAA responsible for satellites in the afternoon orbit and DOD responsible for satellites in the early morning orbit. After that decision, NOAA began developing plans for the Joint Polar Satellite System (JPSS). In October 2011, the JPSS program successfully launched the Suomi National Polar-orbiting Partnership (S-NPP) demonstration satellite, the first in a series of satellites to be launched as part of NOAA's JPSS program.

Given your interest in the progress NOAA has made on the JPSS program, our objectives were to (1) evaluate NOAA's progress in meeting program objectives of sustaining the continuity of the polar-orbiting satellite system through the S-NPP and JPSS satellites, (2) evaluate the quality of the JPSS program schedule, and (3) assess NOAA's plans to address potential gaps in polar satellite data.

To evaluate NOAA's progress in meeting its program objectives, we analyzed plans and reports on the satellites' system development efforts and on the maturity of S-NPP products. We compared current requirements to prior iterations to assess how recent changes in capabilities have impacted program goals and objectives. We also interviewed JPSS program officials to discuss S-NPP product development, JPSS system development, and changes in requirements for JPSS satellites. To evaluate the quality of NOAA's program schedule, we used an exposure draft of GAO's Schedule Assessment Guide[1] to assess component contractor schedules as well as the program's schedule risk analysis and interviewed cognizant JPSS program office and contractor officials. To assess NOAA's plans to address potential gaps in polar satellite data, we compared NOAA's gap mitigation plan and contracted alternatives study against risk mitigation and contingency best practices from GAO and advocated by leading organizations,[2] determined planning shortfalls and key remaining activities for NOAA to accomplish, and interviewed NOAA headquarters and JPSS program officials about their plans.

We conducted this performance audit from October 2012 through September 2013 in accordance with generally accepted government auditing standards. Those standards require that we plan and perform the audit to obtain sufficient, appropriate evidence to provide a reasonable basis for our findings and conclusions based on our audit objectives. Additional details on our objectives, scope, and methodology are provided in appendix I.

---

[1] GAO Schedule Assessment Guide: Best Practices for Project Schedules, GAO-12-120G (exposure draft) (Washington, D.C.: May 30, 2012).

[2] See GAO, Year 2000 Computing Crisis: Business Continuity and Contingency Planning, GAO/AIMD-10.1.19 (Washington, D.C.: August 1998); National Institute of Standards and Technology, Contingency Planning Guide for Federal Information Systems, NIST 800-34 (May 2010); Software Engineering Institute, CMMI® for Acquisition, Version 1.3 (Pittsburgh, Pa.: November 2010).

Background

Since the 1960s, the United States has operated two separate operational polar-orbiting meteorological satellite systems: the Polar-orbiting Operational Environmental Satellite (POES) series, which is managed by NOAA, and the Defense Meteorological Satellite Program (DMSP), which is managed by the Air Force.[3] These satellites obtain environmental data that are processed to provide graphical weather images and specialized weather products. These satellite data are also the predominant input to numerical weather prediction models, which are a primary tool for forecasting weather days in advance—including forecasting the path and intensity of hurricanes. The weather products and models are used to predict the potential impact of severe weather so that communities and emergency managers can help prevent and mitigate its effects. Polar satellites also provide data used to monitor environmental phenomena, such as ozone depletion and drought conditions, as well as data sets that are used by researchers for a variety of studies such as climate monitoring.

Unlike geostationary satellites, which maintain a fixed position relative to the earth, polar-orbiting satellites constantly circle the earth in an almost north-south orbit, providing global coverage of conditions that affect the weather and climate. Each satellite makes about 14 orbits a day. As the earth rotates beneath it, each satellite views the entire earth's surface twice a day. Currently, there is one operational POES satellite and two operational DMSP satellites that are positioned so that they cross the equator in the early morning, midmorning, and early afternoon. In addition, the government relies on a European satellite, called the Meteorological Operational (MetOp) satellite, for satellite observations in the midmorning orbit.[4] In addition to the operational satellites, NOAA, the Air Force, and a European weather satellite organization maintain older satellites that still collect some data and are available to provide limited backup to the operational satellites should they degrade or fail. The last POES satellite was launched in February 2009. The Air Force plans to

---

[3] NOAA provides command and control for both the POES and DMSP satellites after they are in orbit.

[4] The European Organisation for the Exploitation of Meteorological Satellites' MetOp program is a series of three polar-orbiting satellites dedicated to operational meteorology. MetOp satellites are planned to be flown sequentially over 14 years. The first of these satellites was launched in 2006, the second was launched in 2012, and the final satellite in the series is expected to launch in 2017.

launch its two remaining DMSP satellites as needed. Figure 1 illustrates the current operational polar satellite constellation.

Figure 1: Configuration of Operational Polar Satellites

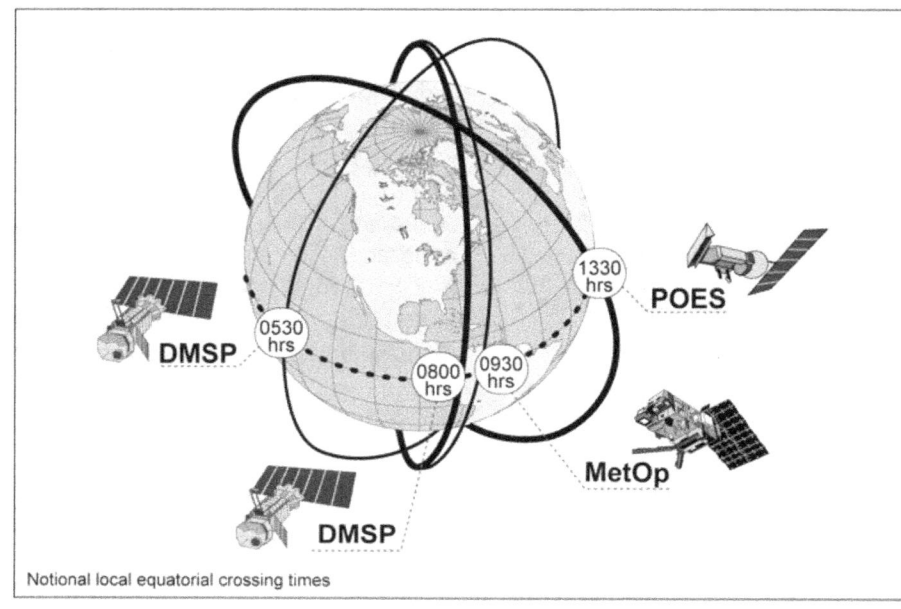

Notional local equatorial crossing times

Sources: GAO, based on NPOESS Integrated Program Office and DOD data, Map Resources (globe).

Polar Satellite Data and Products

Polar satellites gather a broad range of data that are transformed into a variety of products. Satellite sensors observe different bands of radiation wavelengths, called channels, which are used for remotely determining information about the earth's atmosphere, land surface, oceans, and the space environment. When first received, satellite data are considered raw data. To make them usable, processing centers format the data so that they are time-sequenced and include earth-location and calibration information. After formatting, these data are called raw data records. The centers further process these raw data records into channel-specific data sets, called sensor data records and temperature data records. These data records are then used to derive weather and climate products called environmental data records. These environmental data records include a wide range of atmospheric products detailing cloud coverage, temperature, humidity, and ozone distribution; land surface products showing snow cover, vegetation, and land use; ocean products depicting sea surface temperatures, sea ice, and wave height; and

GAO-13-676 Polar-orbiting Environmental Satellites

characterizations of the space environment. Combinations of these data records (raw, sensor, temperature, and environmental data records) are also used to derive more sophisticated products, including outputs from numerical weather models and assessments of climate trends. Figure 2 is a simplified depiction of the various stages of satellite data processing, and figure 3 depicts examples of two different weather products.

Figure 2: Stages of Satellite Data Processing

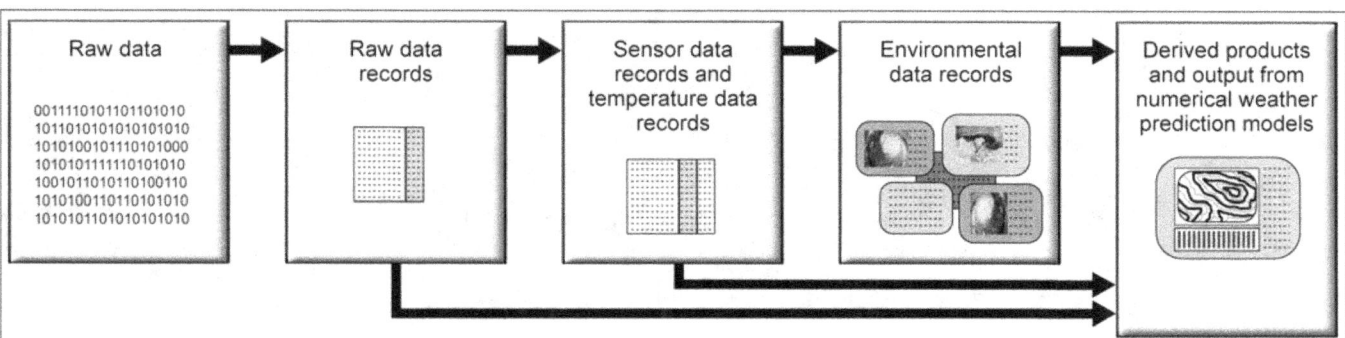

Source: GAO analysis of NOAA information.

Figure 3: Examples of Weather Products

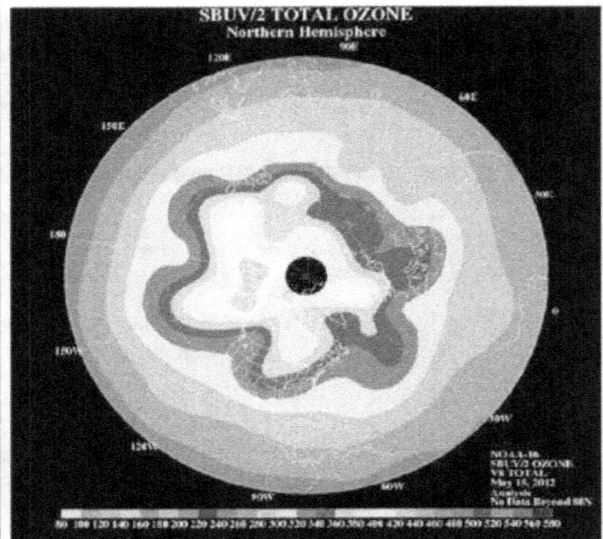

Source: NOAA's National Environmental Satellite Data and Information Service.

Note: The figure on the left is a POES Image of Hurricane Katrina in 2005; the figure on the right is an analysis of ozone concentration produced from POES satellite data.

The NPOESS Program: Inception, Challenges, and Divergence

With the expectation that combining the POES and DMSP programs would reduce duplication and result in sizable cost savings, a May 1994 Presidential Decision Directive required NOAA and DOD to converge the two satellite programs into a single satellite program—NPOESS—capable of satisfying both civilian and military requirements.[5] The converged program, NPOESS, was considered critical to the nation's ability to maintain the continuity of data required for weather forecasting and global climate monitoring. NPOESS satellites were expected to replace the POES and DMSP satellites in the morning, midmorning, and afternoon orbits when they neared the end of their expected life spans.

To manage this program, DOD, NOAA, and NASA formed a tri-agency Integrated Program Office, with NOAA responsible for overall program management for the converged system and for satellite operations, the Air Force responsible for acquisition, and NASA responsible for facilitating

---

[5] Presidential Decision Directive NSTC-2, May 5, 1994.

the development and incorporation of new technologies into the converged system.

When the primary NPOESS contract was awarded in August 2002, the program was estimated to cost about $7 billion through 2018. The program was to include the procurement and launch of 6 satellites over the life of the program, with each satellite hosting a subset of 13 instruments. The planned instruments included 11 environmental sensors, and two systems supporting specific user services (see table 1). To reduce the risk involved in developing new technologies and to maintain climate data continuity, the program planned to launch the demonstration satellite in May 2006.[6] This satellite was intended to demonstrate the functionality of selected instruments that would later be included on the NPOESS satellites. The first NPOESS satellite was to be available for launch in March 2008.

Table 1: Anticipated NPOESS Instruments, as of July 2002

Instrument	Instrument type	Description
Advanced technology microwave sounder (ATMS)	Environmental sensor	Measures microwave energy released and scattered by the atmosphere; to be used in combination with the cross-track infrared sounder to produce daily global atmospheric temperature, humidity, and pressure profiles.
Aerosol polarimetry sensor	Environmental sensor	Retrieves specific aerosol (liquid droplets or solid particles suspended in the atmosphere, such as sea spray, smog, and smoke) and cloud measurements.
Conical microwave imager/sounder	Environmental sensor	Collects microwave images and data needed to measure rain rate, ocean surface wind speed and direction, amount of water in the clouds, and soil moisture, as well as temperature and humidity at different atmospheric levels.
Cross-track infrared sounder (CrIS)	Environmental sensor	Collects measurements of the infrared radiation emitted and scattered by the Earth and atmosphere to determine the vertical distribution of temperature, moisture, and pressure in the atmosphere.
Data collection system	System providing services to users	Collects environmental data from platforms around the world and delivers them to users worldwide.
Earth radiation budget sensor	Environmental sensor	Measures solar short-wave radiation and long-wave radiation released by the Earth back into space on a worldwide scale to enhance long-term climate studies.

---

[6] Originally called the NPOESS Preparatory Project, in January 2012, the satellite's name was changed to the Suomi National Polar-orbiting Partnership satellite.

Instrument	Instrument type	Description
Global positioning system occultation sensor	Environmental sensor	Measures the refraction of radio wave signals from the Global Positioning System and Russia's Global Navigation Satellite System to characterize the ionosphere and information related to the vertical distribution of temperature and moisture of the atmosphere.
Ozone mapper/ profiler suite (OMPS)	Environmental sensor	Collects data needed to measure the amount and distr bution of ozone in the Earth's atmosphere. Consists of two components (nadir and limb) that can be provided separately.
Radar altimeter	Environmental sensor	Measures variances in sea surface height/topography and ocean surface roughness, which are used to determine sea surface height, significant wave height, and ocean surface wind speed and to provide critical inputs to ocean forecasting and climate prediction models.
Search and rescue satellite-aided tracking system	System providing services to users	A subsystem that detects and locates aviators, mariners, and land-based users in distress.
Space environmental sensor suite	Environmental sensor	Collects data to identify, reduce, and predict the effects of space weather on technological systems, including satellites and radio links.
Total and spectral solar irradiance sensor	Environmental sensor	Monitors and captures total and spectral solar irradiance data.
Visible/infrared imager radiometer suite (VIIRS)	Environmental sensor	Collects images and radiometric data used to provide information on the Earth's clouds, atmosphere, ocean, and land surfaces.

Source: GAO analysis of data from the former NPOESS Integrated Program Office.

In the years after the program was initiated, NPOESS encountered significant technical challenges in sensor development, program cost growth, and schedule delays. By November 2005, we estimated that the program's cost had grown to $10 billion, and the schedule for the first launch was delayed by almost 2 years.[7] These issues led to a 2006 decision to restructure the program, which reduced the program's functionality by decreasing the number of planned satellites from 6 to 4, and the number of instruments from 13 to 9. As part of the decision, officials decided to reduce the number of orbits from three (early morning, midmorning, and afternoon) to two (early morning and afternoon) and to rely solely on the European satellites for midmorning orbit data.

Even after the restructuring, however, the program continued to encounter technical issues in developing two sensors, significant tri-

---

[7] GAO, *Polar-orbiting Operational Environmental Satellites: Technical Problems, Cost Increases, and Schedule Delays Trigger Need for Difficult Trade-off Decisions*, GAO-06-249T (Washington, D.C.: Nov. 16, 2005).

agency management challenges, schedule delays, and further cost increases. Because the schedule delays could lead to satellite data gaps, in March 2009 agency executives decided to use S-NPP as an operational satellite.[8] Later, in August 2009, faced with costs that were expected to reach about $15 billion and launch schedules that were delayed by over 5 years, the Executive Office of the President formed a task force, led by the Office of Science and Technology Policy, to investigate the management and acquisition options that would improve the NPOESS program. As a result of this review, in February 2010, the Director of the Office of Science and Technology Policy announced that NOAA and DOD would no longer jointly procure the NPOESS satellite system; instead each agency would plan and acquire its own satellite system.[9] Specifically, NOAA would be responsible for the afternoon orbit and the observations planned for the first and third satellites. DOD would be responsible for the early morning orbit and the observations planned for the second and fourth satellites. The partnership with the European satellite agencies for the midmorning orbit was to continue as planned. When this decision was announced, NOAA and NASA immediately began planning for a new satellite program in the afternoon orbit called JPSS. DOD began planning for a new satellite program in the morning orbit, called the Defense Weather Satellite System, but later decided to terminate the program and reassess its requirements, as directed by Congress.

Overview of Initial NOAA Plans for the JPSS Program

After the decision was made to disband the NPOESS program in 2010, NOAA began the JPSS satellite program. Key plans included:

- relying on NASA for system acquisition, engineering, and integration;
- completing, launching, and supporting S-NPP;
- acquiring and launching two satellites for the afternoon orbit, called JPSS-1 and JPSS-2;
- developing and integrating five sensors on the two satellites;
- finding alternative host satellites for selected instruments that would not be accommodated on the JPSS satellites; and

---

[8] Using S-NPP as an operational satellite means that the satellite's data will be used to provide climate and weather products.

[9] The announcement accompanied the release of the President's fiscal year 2011 budget request.

- providing ground system support for S-NPP, JPSS, and the Defense Weather Satellite System; data communications for MetOp and DMSP; and data processing for NOAA's use of microwave data from an international satellite.

In 2010, NOAA estimated that the life cycle costs of the JPSS program would be approximately $11.9 billion for a program lasting through fiscal year 2024, which included $2.9 billion in NOAA funds spent on NPOESS through fiscal year 2010.[10] Subsequently, the agency undertook a cost estimating exercise where it validated that the cost of the full set of JPSS functions from fiscal year 2012 through fiscal year 2028 would be $11.3 billion. After adding the agency's sunk costs, which had increased to $3.3 billion through fiscal year 2011, the program's life cycle cost estimate totaled $14.6 billion.[11] This amount was $2.7 billion higher than the $11.9 billion estimate for JPSS when NPOESS was disbanded in 2010.

In working with the Office of Management and Budget to establish the president's fiscal year 2013 budget request, NOAA officials stated that they agreed to cap the JPSS life cycle cost at $12.9 billion through 2028, to fund JPSS at roughly $900 million per year through 2017, and to merge funding for two climate sensors into the JPSS budget. Because this cap was $1.7 billion below the expected $14.6 billion life cycle cost of the full program, NOAA decided to remove selected elements from the satellite program. Table 2 compares the planned cost, schedule, and scope of NOAA's satellite programs at different points in time.

---

[10] This figure does not include approximately $2.9 billion in sunk costs that DOD spent on NPOESS through fiscal year 2010.

[11] NOAA's $3.3 billion sunk costs included $2.9 billion through fiscal year 2010 and about $400 million in fiscal year 2011.

Table 2: A Comparison of NPOESS and JPSS, at Different Points in Time

Key area	NPOESS program before it was restructured (as of May 2006)	NPOESS program after it was restructured (as of June 2006)	NPOESS program prior to being disbanded (as of February 2010)	JPSS program (as of May 2010)	JPSS program (as of June 2012)
Life cycle range	1995-2020	1995-2026	1995-2026	1995-2024	1995-2028
Estimated life cycle cost	$8.4 billion	$12.5 billion	$13.95+ billion[a]	$11.9 billion (which includes about $2.9 billion spent through fiscal year 2010 on NPOESS)	$12.9 billion (which includes about $3.3 billion spent through fiscal year 2011 on NPOESS and JPSS)
Number of satellites	6 (in addition to S-NPP)	4 (in addition to S-NPP)	4 (in addition to S-NPP)	2 (in addition to S-NPP)	2 (in addition to S-NPP)
Number of orbits	3 (early morning, midmorning, afternoon)	2 (early morning and afternoon; would rely on European satellites for midmorning orbit data)	2 (early morning and afternoon; would rely on European satellites for midmorning orbit data)	1 (afternoon orbit) (DOD and European satellites would provide early and midmorning orbits, respectively)	1 (afternoon orbit) (DOD and European satellites would provide early and midmorning orbits, respectively)
Launch schedule	S-NPP by October 2006 First NPOESS (C1) by November 2009 Second NPOESS (C2) by June 2011	S-NPP by January 2010 C1 by January 2013 C2 by January 2016 C3 by January 2018 C4 by January 2020	S-NPP no earlier than September 2011 C1 by March 2014 C2 by May 2016 C3 by January 2018 C4 by January 2020	S-NPP—no earlier than September 2011 JPSS-1 available in 2015 JPSS-2 available in 2018	S-NPP—successfully launched in October 2011 JPSS-1 by March 2017 JPSS-2 by December 2022
Number of sensors	11 sensors and 2 user services systems	S-NPP: 4 sensors C1: 6 sensors C2: 2 sensors C3: 6 sensors C4: 2 sensors	S-NPP: 5 sensors C1: 7 sensors[b] C2: 2 sensors C3: 6 sensors C4: 2 sensors	S-NPP: 5 sensors JPSS-1: 5 sensors[c] JPSS-2: 5 sensors	S-NPP: 5 sensors JPSS-1: 5 sensors[c] JPSS-2: 5 sensors Free flyer-1: 3 sensors[d] Free flyer-2: 3 sensors

Source: GAO analysis of NOAA, DOD, and task force data.

[a]Although the program baseline was $13.95 billion in February 2010, we estimated in June 2009 that this cost could grow by about $1 billion. In addition, officials from the Executive Office of the President stated that they reviewed life cycle cost estimates from DOD and the NPOESS program office of $15.1 billion and $16.45 billion, respectively.

[b]In May 2008, the NPOESS Executive Committee approved an additional sensor—the Total and Spectral Solar Irradiance Sensor—for the C1 satellite.

[c]The five sensors are ATMS, the Clouds and the Earth's Radiant Energy System (CERES), CrIS, OMPS, and VIIRS. NOAA also committed to finding an alternative spacecraft and launch accommodation for the Total and Spectral Solar Irradiance Sensor, the Advanced Data Collection System, and the Search and Rescue Satellite-Aided Tracking system.

[d]NOAA planned to launch two stand-alone satellites, called free flyer satellites, to accommodate the Total and Spectral Solar Irradiance Sensor, Search and Rescue Satellite-Aided Tracking system, and an Advanced Data Collection System.

Prior GAO Work Recommended Actions to Address the Risk of Gaps in Polar Satellite Data

We have issued a series of reports on the NPOESS and JPSS programs highlighting technical issues, cost growth, and key management challenges affecting the tri-agency program structure.[12] In June 2012, we reported that while NOAA officials communicated publicly and often about the risk of a polar satellite data gap, the agency had not established plans to mitigate the gap.[13] At the time, NOAA officials stated that the agency would continue to use existing satellites as long as they provide data and that there were no viable alternatives to the JPSS program. However, our report noted that a more comprehensive mitigation plan was essential since it is possible that other governmental, commercial, or foreign satellites could supplement the polar satellite data. Because it could take time to adapt ground systems to receive, process, and disseminate an alternative satellite's data, we noted that any delays in establishing mitigation plans could leave the agency little time to leverage its alternatives. We recommended that NOAA establish mitigation plans for risks associated with pending satellite gaps in the afternoon orbit as well as potential gaps in the early morning and midmorning orbits. NOAA agreed with the report's recommendation and noted that the National Environmental Satellite, Data, and Information Service—a NOAA component agency—had performed analyses on how to mitigate potential gaps in satellite data and planned to provide a report by August 2012.

More recently, in February 2013, we added the potential gap in weather satellite data to our biennial High-Risk list.[14] In that report, we noted that satellite data gaps in the morning or afternoon polar orbits would lead to less accurate and timely weather forecasting; as a result, advanced warning of extreme events would be affected. Such extreme events could include hurricanes, storm surges, and floods. For example, the National

---

[12] See, for example, GAO, *Polar Satellites: Agencies Need to Address Potential Gaps in Weather and Climate Data Coverage*, GAO-11-945T (Washington, D.C.: Sept. 23, 2011); *Polar-orbiting Environmental Satellites: Agencies Must Act Quickly to Address Risks That Jeopardize the Continuity of Weather and Climate Data*, GAO-10-558 (Washington, D.C.: May 27, 2010); *Polar-orbiting Environmental Satellites: With Costs Increasing and Data Continuity at Risk, Improvements Needed in Tri-Agency Decision Making*, GAO-09-772T (Washington, D.C.: June 17, 2009); and *Polar-orbiting Environmental Satellites: With Costs Increasing and Data Continuity at Risk, Improvements Needed in Tri-Agency Decision Making*, GAO-09-564 (Washington, D.C.: June 17, 2009).

[13] GAO, *Polar-orbiting Operational Environmental Satellites: Changing Requirements, Technical Issues, and Looming Data Gaps Require Focused Attention*, GAO-12-604 (Washington, D.C.: June 15, 2012).

[14] GAO, *High-Risk Series: An Update*, GAO-13-283 (Washington, D.C.: February 2013).

GAO-13-676 Polar-orbiting Environmental Satellites

Weather Service performed case studies to demonstrate how its forecasts would have been affected if there were no polar satellite data in the afternoon orbit, and noted that its forecasts for the "Snowmaggedon" winter storm that hit the Mid-Atlantic coast in February 2010 would have predicted a less intense storm further east, with about half of the precipitation at 3, 4, and 5 days before the event. Specifically, the models would have under-forecasted the amount of snow by at least 10 inches. Similarly, a European weather organization[15] recently reported that NOAA's forecasts of Hurricane Sandy's track could have been hundreds of miles off without polar-orbiting satellites—rather than identifying the New Jersey landfall within 30 miles 4 days before landfall, the models would have shown the storm remaining at sea. Such degradation in forecasts and warnings would place lives, property, and our nation's critical infrastructure in danger.

We reported that the length of an afternoon polar satellite data gap could span from 17 months to 3 years or more. In one scenario, S-NPP would last its full expected 5-year life (to October 2016), and JPSS-1 would launch as soon as possible (in March 2017) and undergo on-orbit checkout for a year (until March 2018). In that case, the data gap would extend 17 months. In another scenario, S-NPP would last only 3 years as noted by NASA managers concerned with the workmanship of selected S-NPP sensors. Assuming that the JPSS-1 launch occurred in March 2017 and the satellite data were certified for official use by March 2018, this gap would extend for 41 months. Of course, any problems with JPSS-1 development could delay the launch date and extend the gap period. Figure 4 depicts four possible gap scenarios.

---

[15] The European Centre for Medium Range Weather Forecasts is an independent, intergovernmental organization supported by 34 European nations, providing global medium-to-extended range forecasts.

Figure 4: Potential Gaps in Polar Satellite Data in the Afternoon Orbit

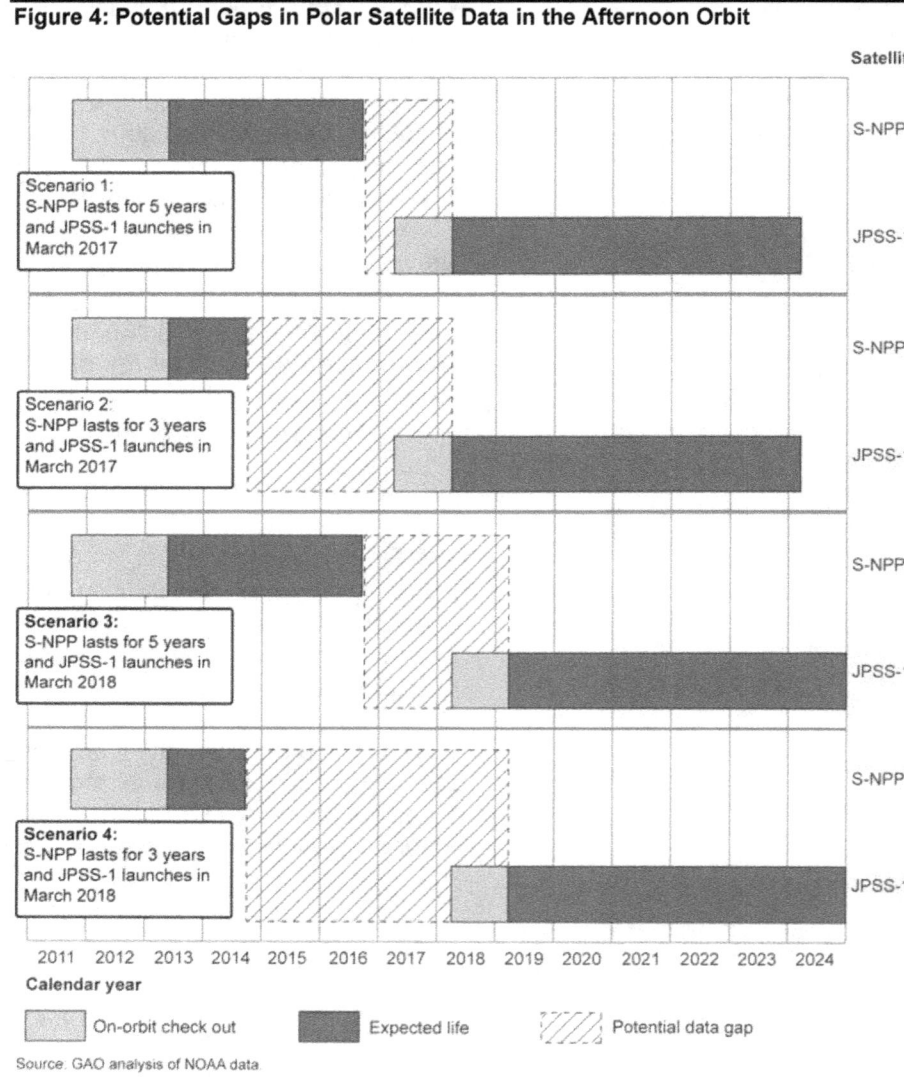

Source: GAO analysis of NOAA data

We also noted that NOAA had recently established a mitigation plan for a potential 14- to 18-month gap in the afternoon orbit, which identified and prioritized options for obtaining critical observations, including alternative satellite data sources and improvements to data assimilation in models and listed technical, programmatic, and management steps needed to implement these options. However, these plans were only a beginning. We suggested that NOAA must make difficult decisions on which steps it would implement to ensure that its mitigation plans are viable when needed, including how these plans would be integrated with the agency's broader end-to-end plans for sustaining weather forecasting capabilities.

NOAA Has Made Progress on JPSS Development, but Continues to Face Challenges in Completing S-NPP Products, Revising the Program's Scope, and Meeting Schedules

NOAA has made progress towards JPSS program objectives of sustaining the continuity of NOAA's polar-orbiting satellite capabilities through the S-NPP, JPSS-1, and JPSS-2 satellites by (1) delivering S-NPP data to weather forecasters and (2) by completing significant instrument and spacecraft development for the JPSS-1 satellite. However, the program is behind schedule in validating the readiness of S-NPP products and has experienced delays on the ground system schedules for the JPSS-1 satellite. Moreover, the program is moving to revise its scope and objectives to reduce costs and prioritize NOAA's weather mission. Until it addresses challenges in product and ground system development, the program office may continue to experience delays in delivering actionable S-NPP data to users and in meeting program development schedules.

Weather Forecasters Are Using Selected S-NPP Products, but the JPSS Program Is Behind Schedule in Validating Products and Unaware of the Full Extent to Which They Are Being Used

In order to sustain polar-orbiting earth observation capabilities through the S-NPP satellite, over the past 18 months the JPSS program had planned to complete activation and commissioning of the S-NPP satellite, transition the satellite from interim to routine operations, and deliver 76 data products that were precise enough for use in operational weather observations and forecasts. To develop the precise data products, NOAA established a process for calibrating and validating its products. Under this process, most products (which are primarily sensor data records and environmental data records) proceed through three different levels of algorithm maturity—the beta, provisional, and validated levels.[16] NOAA had originally planned to complete efforts to validate S-NPP products by October 2013, which was 2 years after the S-NPP satellite was launched. It is not enough, however, to simply deliver validated products. Both the Software Engineering Institute and GAO recommend tracking whether customers are receiving the expected value from products once they are

---

[16] According to NOAA and NASA officials, the products go through a beta stage (in which products have been minimally validated, but are available to users so that they can begin working with the data); a provisional stage (in which products are not optimal, but are ready for operational evaluation by users); and a validated stage (in which products are ready for operational use).

deployed, and whether corrective actions are needed.[17] Moreover, in April 2013 the Executive Office of the President's National Science and Technology Council released a national strategy for civil earth observations that called for agencies to, among other things, track the extent to which earth observation data are actually being used, track whether the data had an impact, and provide data users a mechanism to provide feedback regarding ease of use, suspected quality issues, and other aspects of the data.[18]

The JPSS program has made progress on S-NPP since launching the satellite in October 2011. Specifically, the program completed satellite activation and commissioning in March 2012, and transitioned from interim operations under NASA to routine operations under NOAA in February 2013. The program also made key upgrades to the ground system supporting S-NPP. For example, in November 2012 the office completed an interim backup command and control facility that could protect the health and safety of the satellite if unexpected issues occurred at the primary mission operations facility. In addition, the JPSS program office has been working to calibrate and validate S-NPP products in order to make them precise enough for use in weather-related operations.

While the program office plans to have 18 products validated for operational use by September 2013, it is behind schedule for the other products. Specifically, the program expects to complete validating 35 S-NPP products by the end of September 2014 and 1 other product by the end of September 2015, almost 1 and 2 years later than originally planned. In addition, the program office reported that 15 products do not need to be validated, one product's validation date has not been established, and 6 products do not have estimated validation dates because the program plans to remove them from its requirements. The program categorized its products by their priority, ranging from priority-1 for the highest priority products, to priority-4 for the lowest priority products. According to NOAA and NASA officials, the S-NPP products' validation has been delayed in part because of issues initially identified on

---

[17] Software Engineering Institute, CMMI® for Acquisition, Version 1.3 (Pittsburgh, Pa.: November 2010) and GAO, Information Technology Investment Management: A Framework for Assessing and Improving Process Maturity, Version 1.1, GAO-04-394G (Washington, D.C.: March 2004).

[18] Executive Office of the President National Science and Technology Council, National Strategy for Civil Earth Observations (Washington, D.C.: April 2013).

VIIRS that had to be corrected and additional time needed to validate environmental data record products that require observations of seasonal weather phenomena. Further, program officials stated that they rebaselined the planned product validation timelines in November 2011 and have been generally meeting the target dates of this revised plan. Table 3 illustrates program-reported data on the number of products in each priority level, examples of products, and the estimated validation date for the last product at each level.

Table 3: Estimated Completion Dates for S-NPP Products, as of July 2013

Number of products	Priority level (number of products)	Examples of products	Validated by
18	Priority 1 or 2: 4	ATMS land surface emissivity Advanced Microwave Scanning Radiometer-2 sensor data record VIIRS polar winds VIIRS vegetation fraction	End of September 2013
	Priority 3 or 4: 14	ATMS rainfall rate OMPS-nadir profile ozone OMPS-nadir ozone total column Advanced Microwave Scanning Radiometer-2 cloud liquid water	
35	Priority 1 or 2: 5	ATMS sensor data record CrIS sensor data record VIIRS sensor data record VIIRS imagery	End of September 2014
	Priority 3 or 4: 29	OMPS-nadir sensor data record VIIRS active fires VIIRS cloud optical thickness CrIS infrared ozone profile	
	No priority: 1	VIIRS ocean color/chlorophyll	
1	Priority 3 or 4: 1	VIIRS vegetation health index suite	End of September 2015
15	Priority not assigned	Application packets and raw data records	Not applicable[a]
1	Priority 1 or 2: 1	Advanced Microwave Scanning Radiometer-2 temperature data record	Date is still to be determined
6	Priority 1 or 2: 0	Not applicable	Planned to be removed from requirements[b]
	Priority 3 or 4: 5	CERES sensor data record	
	No priority: 1	OMPS-limb profiler sensor data record	

Source: GAO analysis of NOAA documents.

Notes:

[a]Program officials stated that selected products, including raw data records and application packets, do not undergo validation.

[b]Program officials expect that these requirements will be removed once the transfer of instruments is approved through the fiscal year 2014 budget process.

Even though S-NPP products are not at the validated stage in which products are ready for operational use, the National Weather Service (NWS) has accepted certain products for use in its operational systems. For example, the JPSS program office reported that NWS is using ATMS temperature data records in its operational forecasts, and that the Alaska

Weather Forecast Offices are using VIIRS imagery in its forecasts. In addition, NWS's National Centers for Environmental Prediction is evaluating CrIS sensor data records for use in numerical weather prediction, but has not yet used the data operationally because it is in the midst of a computer upgrade. Officials also stated that the program obtains information on the operational use of S-NPP data from other NOAA offices, including the National Ocean Service and the National Marine and Fisheries Service.

While NOAA is aware of these uses, it does not track the extent to which key satellite data users—including users from the Air Force, Navy, Forest Service, European weather offices, and academic institutions—have incorporated S-NPP data into their operations or if corrective actions are needed to make the products more accurate or more effective for the specific users. Program officials noted that they are not required to tailor products to meet non-NOAA user requirements, and that they do not have a tracking mechanism that would allow them to identify which entities are using the data. They noted, however, that the program obtains informal reports from customer representatives through various working groups and forums, such as the Low-earth Orbiting Requirements Working Group and the JPSS Customer Forum. While these efforts obtain information from known customer groups, they do not meet best practices for actively tracking whether customers are using the products, receiving the expected value, or in need of product corrections. Until the program office tracks the use of S-NPP and future JPSS products, it will not have full knowledge of the extent to which products are being used to assess the value they provide to end users and whether corrective actions are needed. More significantly, without information on who is using S-NPP data, NOAA will be unable to ensure that the significant investment made on this satellite is not wasted.

Development of JPSS Flight Project Is on Track, but Scheduling Issues on the Ground System Have Caused Delays

In order to sustain polar-orbiting earth observation capabilities, the program is working to complete development of the JPSS-1 systems in preparation for a March 2017 launch date. To manage this initiative, the program office organized its responsibilities into two separate projects: (1) the flight project, which includes sensors, spacecraft, and launch vehicles and (2) the ground project, which includes ground-based data processing and command and control systems. Table 4 shows the JPSS projects and their key components.

Table 4: JPSS Projects and Components

Project	Key components and responsibilities
Flight	Sensors: ATMS, CERES, CrIS, OMPS, VIIRS
	Spacecraft
	Launch vehicle
Ground	Satellite command, control, and communications
	Interface data processing segment

Source: NOAA's JPSS program office.

JPSS projects and components are at various stages of system development. The flight project has nearly completed instrument hardware development for the JPSS-1 satellite and has begun testing certain instruments. Also, the flight project completed a major design review for the JPSS-1 satellite's spacecraft. While the flight project's development is on track, the ground project experienced delays in its planned schedule that could further delay major program milestones, including key reviews required to establish the program's cost and schedule baseline.

Flight Project: JPSS-1 Instrument and Spacecraft Development Is On Track

The flight project is generally on track with respect to planned JPSS-1 instrument and spacecraft development efforts. According to program reports of instrument development, the instruments for the JPSS-1 satellite are nearly complete. Specifically, as of July 2013, the instrument hardware ranged from 80 to 100 percent complete. Also, all of the instruments have completed or are scheduled to complete environmental testing reviews in 2013 and are to be delivered to the spacecraft by 2014. The spacecraft completed its critical design review—which evaluates whether the design is appropriately mature to continue with the final design and fabrication—in January 2013.

While individual instruments have experienced delays, the key testing milestones and delivery dates for the instruments and spacecraft have generally held constant since the last key decision point in July 2012. CERES experienced a 10-month slip in its delivery date due to a technical issue with the instrument's internal calibration monitor, and ATMS experienced an 8-month slip to its pre-environmental review due to an issue in one of the sensor's channels, but even accounting for these slips, the instruments have a schedule reserve of 14 and 10 months, respectively. VIIRS is expected to be the last instrument to be delivered to the spacecraft and has a schedule reserve of 6 months. Also, between July 2012 and December 2012 instrument contractors' estimated costs at completion increased by $29 million for ATMS, CrIS, and OMPS, while the cost for VIIRS decreased by $46 million. In addition, based on program reports of technical performance, the instruments and the spacecraft are generally meeting expected technical performance. Table 5 describes the current status of the components of the JPSS-1 flight project.

Table 5: Status of Key Components of the Flight Project Supporting the JPSS-1 Satellite, as of July 2013

Component	Status
Instrument	
ATMS	The instrument completed its hardware development and is in environmental testing. The instrument experienced a technical issue beginning in November 2012 in which science counts in one of the channels were lower than expected. The program replaced channel components with spares and performed additional regression testing. This issue delayed the planned pre-environmental review by 6 months from November 2012 to May 2013. ATMS is expected to be delivered for integration on the spacecraft in March 2014.
CERES	The instrument completed its hardware development and is in environmental testing. The instrument's internal cal bration monitor exhibited unstable performance during calibration, which delayed its delivery by 13 months. The cause of this issue is still unknown. CERES underwent pre-environmental review in February 2012. The program office plans to perform additional calibration testing, vacuum performance testing, and regression testing prior to its delivery in October 2013.
CrIS	The instrument completed 80 percent of its hardware development and is in subsystem integration. The instrument's electronic components have been experiencing a power-up issue, possibly due to a timing issue with the digital power supply. The program office replaced the power supply with a spare and is working on resolving the issue and completing acceptance testing. Additional work remaining on the instrument includes completing the subsystems, integrating the complete instrument, conducting the pre-environmental review in September 2013, and completing its environmental test program. The expected delivery date for the instrument is August 2014.
OMPS-Nadir	The instrument completed its hardware development and is in environmental testing. The instrument's diffuser experienced degradation during calibration and the adhesive was deemed the root cause. There was no performance impact but the instrument's delivery date slipped 3 months. The program office planned to complete cleaning, regression testing, and preparation of the nadir unit for testing. The instrument completed a pre-environmental review in April 2013, is conducting environmental testing, and is expected to be delivered in August 2014.
VIIRS	The instrument completed 80 percent of its hardware development and is in subsystem integration. Several sensor components have been delivered, installed, and integrated. VIIRS is expected to undergo pre-environmental review in October 2013 with an expected delivery in October 2014.
Spacecraft	The spacecraft completed its critical design review in December 2012; hardware development is ongoing. The spacecraft has an expected delivery in October 2014.
Launch vehicle	NASA awarded a contract for launch services in July 2012. Previously accepted risks for the launch program on S-NPP are being reviewed for applicability and potential mitigation.

Source: GAO analysis of JPSS program office data.

Ground Project: Progress Made, but Facility Scheduling Problems Have Caused Delays

The JPSS ground project has made progress in developing the ground system components, but scheduling issues have caused delays in the deployment of system upgrades. Specifically, between August 2012 and February 2013, the program office defined the ground system's technical performance baseline, ordered and received the first increment of hardware for the next major software release, and transitioned S-NPP operational management from the JPSS program to NOAA's office responsible for satellite operations.

However, the program has delayed the delivery of key ground system upgrades needed to support JPSS-1 because the facilities needed for hardware installation, software development, and testing activities were not available when needed. The ground system upgrades, called block 1.5 and 2.0, were originally scheduled to be delivered in January and December 2015, respectively. To address the problem in scheduling the facilities, NOAA delayed the delivery of block 1.5 and merged it with block 2.0. The program is now expecting to deliver both upgrades in December 2015. We have previously reported that compressing system development schedules introduces program risk because it implies the need to accomplish a larger number of activities in parallel and on time before the next major event can occur as planned.[19] As a result, any complications in the merged ground system upgrades could affect the system's readiness to support the JPSS-1 launch date.

NOAA Revised Program Scope to Focus on Weather Priorities and Reduce Costs

While NOAA is moving forward to complete product development on the S-NPP satellite and system development on the JPSS-1 satellite, the agency recently made major revisions to the program's scope and planned capabilities and is moving to implement other scope changes as it finalizes its plans pending congressional approval. We previously reported that, as part of its fiscal year 2013 budget process, NOAA was considering removing selected elements of the program in order to reduce total program costs from $14.6 billion to $12.9 billion.[20] By October 2012, NOAA made the following changes in the program's scope:

- develop two (instead of three) TSIS instruments as well as two free-flyer spacecraft and launch vehicles to accommodate the instruments;
- reduce the previously planned network of fifteen ground-based receptor stations to two receptor sites at the north pole and two sites at the south pole;

---

[19] See GAO-12-120G (exposure draft).

[20] GAO-12-604.

- increase the time it takes to obtain satellite data and deliver it to the end user from 30 minutes to 80 minutes on the JPSS-2 satellite;[21]
- not install an interface data processing segment at the two Navy locations or at the Air Force Weather Agency; and
- withdraw future support for ground operations for DOD's Defense Weather Satellite System, which was subsequently cancelled.

More recently, as proposed by the administration, NOAA began implementing additional changes in the program's scope and objectives in order to meet the agency's highest-priority needs for weather forecasting and reduce program costs from $12.9 billion to $11.3 billion. Specifically, NOAA has begun to:

- Transfer requirements for building the OMPS-limb and CERES follow-on climate sensors for the JPSS-2 satellite to NASA.
- Transfer the first free-flyer mission from the JPSS program to a separate NOAA program, called the Polar Free Flyer program, and cancel the second free-flyer mission. More information on the Polar Free Flyer program is provided in appendix II.
- Eliminate requirements for a legacy type of broadcast transmitter, which, according to NOAA officials, is in a spectrum range being crowded out by terrestrial users and is consistent with its European partners' plans.
- Reduce science and algorithm requirements for lower-priority data products.
- Reduce operations and sustainment costs based on increased efficiencies through moving from customized components to more off-the-shelf solutions.
- Reduce the mission life cycle by 3 years from 2028 to 2025.

While we were unable to precisely itemize the reductions in costs associated with various program changes, program officials provided rough estimates. The following table summarizes the reported cost reductions associated with key changes to the JPSS program.

---

[21] In January 2013, program officials revised this delay to 96 minutes to more precisely reflect the time it takes to send products from the ground system to the end users.

Table 6: Reported Cost Reductions Associated with JPSS Changes

Timing of revisions	Program reported cost reductions	Major scope changes and other revisions
June 2012	$1.7 billion through 2028 (from the $14.6 billion to $12.9 billion life cycle cost estimates)	Restructured free flyer missions ($800M)
		Revised operations and sustainment concept ($700M)
		Reduced reserve estimates ($200M)
April 2013	$1.6 billion through 2025 (from the $12.9 billion to $11.3 billion life cycle cost estimates)	Transferred first free flyer mission to Polar Free Flyer program and transferred a TSIS, CERES, and OMPS-Limb instrument to NASA ($750M)
		Reduced program lifetime by 3 years, from 2028 to 2025 ($390M)
		Eliminated second free-flyer mission and one type of communication downlink ($240M)
		Lowered expected costs for the JPSS-1 launch vehicle and launch services ($9M)
		Saved in other areas, including costs saved by acquiring VIIRS spare parts from the Air Force and eliminating enhanced data processing of data obtained from the Global Change Observation Mission-Water satellite ($211M)

Source: GAO analysis of JPSS program data.

While there are a number of reasons for individual changes in the program, the key reason for the June 2012 changes was to meet the program's $12.9 billion cost cap. The reasons for the more recent changes were to reduce mission costs and complexity, focus JPSS priorities on NOAA's weather forecasting mission, and identify opportunities to reduce potential gaps between JPSS satellites, all of which an independent study on NOAA's satellite program recommended in July 2012.

While these are worthy goals, the changes NOAA implemented over the last 2 years will have an impact on those who rely on polar satellite data. Specifically, satellite data products will be delivered more slowly than anticipated because of the reduction in the number of ground stations, and military users may not obtain the variety of products once anticipated at the rates anticipated because of the removal of their ground-based processing subsystems. Further, while not as obvious, the impact of other changes, including the removal of the communications downlink and the reduction of requirements for certain algorithms, could also affect specific groups of satellite data users. As NOAA moves to implement these program changes, it will be important to assess and understand the impact the changes will have on satellite data users.

JPSS Schedules Demonstrate Multiple Best Scheduling Practices, but Integration Problems and Other Weaknesses Reduce Confidence in the JPSS-1 Launch Date

The JPSS program office has established a preliminary integrated master schedule and implemented multiple scheduling best practices, but the integrated master schedule is not complete and weaknesses in component schedules significantly reduce the program's schedule quality as well as management's ability to monitor, manage, and forecast satellite launch dates. The incomplete integrated master schedule and shortfalls in component schedules are due in part to the program's plans to further refine the schedule as well as schedule management and reporting requirements that varied among contractors. Further, while the program is reporting a 70 percent confidence level in the JPSS-1 launch date, its analysis is likely to be overly optimistic because it was not conducted with an integrated schedule and included a component schedule with weaknesses. Until the program office completes its integrated master schedule and addresses weaknesses in component schedules, it will lack the information it needs to effectively monitor development progress, manage dependencies between schedules, and forecast the JPSS-1 satellite's completion and launch.

The JPSS Program Has Not Yet Established a Complete Integrated Master Schedule

According to our guidance on best practices in scheduling,[22] the success of a program depends in part on having an integrated and reliable master schedule that defines when and how long work will occur and how each activity is related to the others. The program schedule provides not only a road map for systematic project execution but also the means by which to gauge progress, identify and resolve potential problems, and promote accountability at all levels of the program. An integrated master schedule constitutes a program schedule as a network of logically linked sequences of activities that includes the entire required scope of effort, including the effort necessary from the government, contractors, and other key parties for a program's successful execution from start to finish. Although the integrated master schedule includes all government, contractor, and external effort, the government program management office is ultimately responsible for its development and maintenance.

The JPSS program office provided a preliminary integrated master schedule in June 2013, but this schedule is incomplete. The program's June 2013 schedule is its first attempt to document a programwide integrated master schedule since it began in October 2010. The schedule

---

[22] GAO-12-120G (exposure draft).

contains the scope of work for key program components, such as the JPSS-1 and JPSS-2 satellites and the ground system, and cites linkages to more detailed component schedules. However, significant weaknesses exist in the program's schedule. Specifically, about one-third of the schedule is missing logical relationships called dependencies that are needed to depict the sequence in which activities occur. Because a logic relationship dictates the effect of an on-time, delayed, or accelerated activity on subsequent activities, any missing or incorrect logic relationship is potentially damaging to the entire network. Complete network logic between all activities is essential if the schedule is to correctly forecast the start and end dates of activities within the plan. Program documentation acknowledges that this schedule is not yet complete and the program office plans to refine it over time. Until the program office completes its integrated schedule and includes logically linked sequences of activities, it will lack the information it needs to effectively monitor development progress, manage dependencies, and forecast the JPSS-1 satellite's completion and launch.

The Quality of JPSS-1 Component Schedules Is Inconsistent

Our scheduling guidance identifies ten best practices that support four characteristics of a high-quality, reliable schedule—comprehensive, well-constructed, credible, and controlled.[23] A *comprehensive* schedule includes all government and contractor activities, reflects resources (labor, materials, and overhead) needed to do the work, and realistically reflects how long each activity will take. A *well-constructed* schedule includes activities that are sequenced with the most straightforward logic possible, a critical path[24] that represents a true model of the activities that drive the project's earliest completion date, and total float that accurately depicts schedule flexibility. A *credible* schedule reflects the order of events necessary to achieve aggregated products or outcomes (horizontal traceability) and maps varying levels of the schedule to one another (vertical traceability). Also, a credible schedule includes data about risks and opportunities that are used to predict a level of confidence in meeting the project's completion date. A *controlled* schedule is updated periodically by trained schedulers using actual progress and logic to

---

[23] GAO-12-120G (exposure draft).

[24] The critical path is generally defined as the longest continuous sequence of activities in a schedule. As such, it defines the program's earliest completion date or minimum duration.

realistically forecast dates for program activities and is compared against a designated baseline schedule to measure, monitor, and report the project's progress. The JPSS program office is applying NASA's schedule management handbook guidance to manage its schedules, which is largely consistent with our guidance on scheduling best practices. Table 7 provides more detail on the best practices and key characteristics of a reliable schedule.

Table 7: The Four Characteristics and Ten Best Practices of a High-Quality and Reliable Schedule

Characteristic	Best practice	Description
Comprehensive	Capturing all activities	The schedule should reflect all activities as defined in the project's work breakdown structure, which defines in detail the work necessary to accomplish a project's objectives, including activities both the owner and contractors are to perform.
	Assigning resources to all activities	The schedule should reflect the resources (labor, materials, overhead) needed to do the work, whether they will be available when needed, and any funding or time constraints.
	Establishing the duration of all activities	The schedule should realistically reflect how long each activity will take. When the duration of each activity is determined, the same rationale, historical data, and assumptions used for cost estimating should be used. Durations should be reasonably short and meaningful and allow for discrete progress measurement. Schedules that contain planning and summary planning packages as activities will normally reflect longer durations until broken into work packages or specific activities.
Well-constructed	Sequencing all activities	The schedule should be planned so that critical project dates can be met. To do this, activities need to be logically sequenced—that is, listed in the order in which they are to be carried out. In particular, activities that must be completed before other activities can begin (predecessor activities), as well as activities that cannot begin until other activities are completed (successor activities), should be identified. Date constraints and lags should be minimized and justified. This helps ensure that the interdependence of activities that collectively lead to the completion of events or milestones can be established and used to guide work and measure progress.
	Confirming that the critical path is valid	The schedule should identify the program critical path—the path of longest duration through the sequence of activities. Establishing a valid critical path is necessary for examining the effects of any activity's slipping along this path. The program critical path determines the program's earliest completion date and focuses the team's energy and management's attention on the activities that will lead to the project's success.
	Ensuring reasonable total float	The schedule should identify reasonable float (or slack)—the amount of time by which a predecessor activity can slip before the delay affects the program's estimated finish date—so that the schedule's flexibility can be determined. Large total float on an activity or path indicates that the activity or path can be delayed without jeopardizing the finish date. The length of delay that can be accommodated without the finish date's slipping depends on a variety of factors, including the number of date constraints within the schedule and the amount of uncertainty in the duration estimates, but the activity's total float provides a reasonable estimate of this value. As a general rule, activities along the critical path have the least float.

Characteristic	Best practice	Description
Credible	Verifying that the schedule can be traced horizontally and vertically	The detailed schedule should be horizontally traceable, meaning that it should link products and outcomes associated with other sequenced activities. These links are commonly referred to as "handoffs" and serve to verify that activities are arranged in the right order for achieving aggregated products or outcomes. The integrated master schedule should also be vertically traceable—that is, varying levels of activities and supporting subactivities can be traced. Such mapping or alignment of levels enables different groups to work to the same master schedule.
	Conducting a schedule risk analysis	A schedule risk analysis uses a good critical path method schedule and data about project schedule risks and opportunities as well as statistical simulation to predict the level of confidence in meeting a program's completion date, determine the time contingency needed for a level of confidence, and identify high-priority risks and opportunities. As a result, the baseline schedule should include a buffer or reserve of extra time.
Controlled	Updating the schedule using actual progress and logic	Progress updates and logic provide a realistic forecast of start and completion dates for program activities. Maintaining the integrity of the schedule logic at regular intervals is necessary to reflect the true status of the program. To ensure that the schedule is properly updated, people responsible for the updating should be trained in critical path method scheduling.
	Maintaining a baseline schedule	A baseline schedule is the basis for managing the project scope, the time period for accomplishing it, and the required resources. The baseline schedule is designated the target schedule, subject to a configuration management control process, against which project performance can be measured, monitored, and reported. The schedule should be continually monitored so as to reveal when forecasted completion dates differ from planned dates and whether schedule variances will affect downstream work. A corresponding baseline document explains the overall approach to the project, defines custom fields in the schedule file, details ground rules and assumptions used in developing the schedule, and justifies constraints, lags, long activity durations, and any other unique features of the schedule.

Source: GAO Schedule Assessment Guide, GAO-12-120G (exposure draft).

The quality of three selected component schedules supporting the JPSS-1 mission—VIIRS, the spacecraft, and the ground system—was inconsistent with respect to implementing the characteristics of a high-quality, reliable schedule.[25] Each schedule had strengths and weaknesses with respect to sound scheduling practices, but VIIRS was a stronger schedule with fewer weaknesses compared to the ground system and spacecraft schedules. Since the reliability of an integrated schedule depends in part on the reliability of its subordinate schedules, schedule quality weaknesses in these schedules could transfer to an IMS derived from them. Table 8 identifies the quality of each of the selected JPSS-1 component schedules based on the extent to which they met ten

---

[25] These three component schedules represent the critical path for the flight project and the entire ground system schedule.

best practices of high-quality and reliable schedules; the discussion that follows highlights observed strengths and weaknesses from each schedule. In addition, appendix III includes a more detailed assessment of each schedule against the ten best practices.

Table 8: Assessment of JPSS-1 Component Schedule Quality

Schedule characteristic or best practice	Ground system	Spacecraft	VIIRS
Comprehensive			
Capturing all activities	◕	◑	◕
Assigning resources to all activities	◕	◕	◕
Establishing the duration of all activities	◕	◑	●
Well-constructed			
Sequencing all activities	◕	◑	◕
Confirming that the critical path is valid	◔	◑	◕
Ensuring reasonable total float	◑	◑	◕
Credible			
Verifying that the schedule can be traced horizontally and vertically	◑	◑	◕
Conducting a schedule risk analysis	◔	◑	◑
Controlled			
Updating the schedule using actual progress and logic	◕	◕	●
Maintaining a baseline schedule	◕	◑	◕

Source: GAO analysis of detailed schedules and related documentation for the VIIRS instrument, spacecraft, and ground system.

● = Met: The program office or contractor provided complete evidence that satisfies the entire criterion.

◕ = Substantially met: The program office or contractor provided evidence that satisfies a large portion of the criterion.

◑ = Partially met: The program office or contractor provided evidence that satisfies about half of the criterion.

◔ = Minimally met: The program office or contractor provided evidence that satisfies a small portion of the criterion.

○ = Not met: The program office or contractor provided no evidence that satisfies any of the criterion.

Ground Schedule

Of the ten best practices, the ground system schedule minimally met two best practices, partially met two best practices, and substantially met six best practices. There were strengths in the ground schedule in that the contractor established a clear process for integrated information between the schedule and its resource management software and the contractor has performed resource leveling on the schedule. In addition, the contractor stated that people responsible for the activities estimated activity durations. Also, the contractor stated that it performs wellness checks on the quality of the schedule after each update to identify issues associated with missing logic or date constraints and provides a monthly status briefing to the JPSS program office that addresses the status of external schedule handoffs.

However, there were also weaknesses in the ground schedule. For example, activities on the critical path with date constraints are preventing accurate calculations of the schedule's total float, or flexibility. In order for the critical path to be valid, the activities on the critical path must also have reasonable total float. Without a critical path that accurately calculates schedule flexibility, the program office will not be able to provide reliable timeline estimates or identify when problems or changes may occur and their effect on downstream work. Moreover, while the contractor conducted a schedule risk analysis on the schedule, that analysis was for select near-term milestones rather than the readiness of the ground system for the launch of JPSS-1 and it did not include the risks most likely to delay the project. A schedule risk analysis should be conducted through the finish milestone and should include risk data to determine activities that most often end up on the critical path.

Spacecraft Schedule

Of the ten best practices, the spacecraft schedule partially met eight best practices, and substantially met two best practices. There were strengths in the spacecraft schedule in that it was horizontally and vertically traceable; the contractor provided evidence of monthly progress updates to management, including status reporting of key milestones, handoffs, explanations of date changes, and an analysis of the critical and near-critical paths; the contractor conducted a schedule risk analysis; and the schedule included baseline dates of activities for comparisons of actual performance to date.

However, there were also weaknesses in the spacecraft schedule. For example, the schedule had a low level of detail and included one-third of remaining activities with durations greater than 44 days, even after accounting for undefined and procurement-related activities. When establishing the durations of activities, they should be reasonably short and meaningful and allow for discrete progress measurement. Durations longer than 2 months do not facilitate objective measurement of accomplished effort and the milestone to detail activity ratio does not allow for effective progress measurement and reporting. As another example of a quality shortfall, the schedule was overly flexible with high float values that were not justified in schedule documentation. Specifically, 70 percent of remaining activities had about 5 business weeks of float, including 67 activities that had over 1,000 days of float, meaning that these activities could slip approximately 3.5 years without affecting the project's completion date. In order to establish reasonable total float, there should be documented justification for high float values in the schedule. Without this, it is unclear whether float values are high due to factors accepted by management and which are due to incomplete logic or other issues.

VIIRS Schedule

The VIIRS schedule partially met one best practice, substantially met seven best practices, and fully met two best practices. There were strengths in the VIIRS schedule in that the contractor established a clear process for integrating information between the schedule and resource management software, stated that durations were estimated by the people responsible for the activities based on work to be done, and justified in its schedule documentation activities with durations longer than 44 days. In addition, the contractor justified in schedule documentation the use of all date constraints, identified a valid driving path of activities for managing the program, and identified reasonable float values or justified them to the JPSS program office. Further, the contractor provided a schedule narrative accompanying each status update, which describes the status of key milestone dates (including the program finish date); explanations for changes in key dates; and a description of critical paths.

However, there were also weaknesses in the VIIRS schedule. For example, the schedule had milestones that represented handoffs between contractor integrated product teams, but it did not include handoffs to the JPSS program office. In order to verify a schedule's horizontal traceability, handoffs should link products and outcomes associated with other sequenced activities. Without this, there could be different expectations between management and activity owners. As another example, the contractor conducted a schedule risk analysis with a good schedule network and obtained three different duration estimates from subject matter experts. However, the duration estimates did not reflect risks from the project's risk register and the analysis was focused only on activities on the critical path. This approach is flawed because activities that are not currently on the critical path could become critical as risks occur.

The inconsistency in quality among the three schedules has multiple causes. Program and contractor officials explained that certain weaknesses have been corrected with updated schedules. In other cases, the weaknesses lacked documented explanation in part because the JPSS program office did not require contractors to provide such documentation. Based on program schedule documentation, the schedule management and reporting requirements varied across contractors without documented justification for tailored approaches, which may partially explain the inconsistency in practices among the schedules. Since the reliability of an integrated schedule depends in part on the reliability of its subordinate schedules, schedule quality weaknesses in these schedules will transfer to an integrated master schedule derived from them. Consequently, the extent to which there are quality weaknesses in JPSS-1 support schedules further constrains the program's ability to monitor progress, manage key dependencies, and forecast completion dates. Until the program office addresses the scheduling shortfalls in its component schedules, the JPSS schedule will have lower quality and reduced reliability as a management tool for monitoring and forecasting satellite launch dates.

Program Has Confidence in the JPSS-1 Schedule, but Its Assumptions Do Not Reflect Weaknesses in the Underlying Data

According to our guidance on best practices in scheduling,[26] a schedule risk analysis uses statistical techniques to predict a level of confidence in meeting a program's completion date. This analysis focuses on key risks and how they affect the schedule's activities. The analysis does not focus solely on the critical path because, with risk considered, any activity may potentially affect the program's completion date. By relying on statistical simulations to randomly vary activity durations according to the probability of occurrence for certain durations and risks, the analysis seeks to develop a probability distribution of possible completion dates that reflect the program plan and enable an organization to match a date to its degree of risk tolerance.

The JPSS program office has conducted a schedule risk analysis on the JPSS-1 mission schedule (and launch date) through NASA's joint cost

---

[26] GAO-12-120G (exposure draft).

and schedule confidence level (JCL) process.[27] The JCL implemented by the JPSS program office represents a best practice in schedule management for establishing a credible schedule and reflects a robust schedule risk analysis conducted on key JPSS-1 schedule components. For example, the analysis assessed the impacts of key risks from the risk register and how multiple duration estimates for activities, based on documented uncertainty distributions, could affect the schedule. Based on the results of the JCL, the program office reports that its level of confidence in the JPSS-1 schedule is 70 percent and that it has sufficient schedule reserve to maintain a launch date of no later than March 2017.

However, the program office's level of confidence in the JPSS-1 schedule may be overly optimistic for two key reasons. First, the model that the program office used was based on flight project activities rather than an integrated schedule consisting of flight, ground, program office, and other activities relevant to the development and launch of JPSS-1. As a result, the JPSS program office's confidence level projections do not factor in the ongoing scheduling issues that are impacting the ground project. Had those issues been considered, the JPSS-1 confidence level would have been lower. Second, there are concerns regarding the spacecraft schedule's quality as discussed in the previous section. Factoring in these concerns, the confidence of the JPSS-1 satellite's schedule and projected launch date would be lower. We have previously reported that when using the JCL, NASA projects did not always include relevant cost and risk inputs.[28]

While program officials noted that they included key ground system risks in their calculations, they did not include ground system scope in the JCL because it was too difficult to allocate ground system components to individual missions. Moreover, officials stated that they do not plan to include ground project or program office activities in future JCL updates. While it may have been difficult to include ground system scope in the JCL, without this, the program's schedule risk analysis and JCL do not reflect the full amount of work to be performed leading to JPSS-1 launch.

---

[27] The JCL is a probabilistic analysis that includes, among other things, all cost and schedule elements, incorporates and quantifies potential risks, assesses the impacts of cost and schedule to date, and addresses available annual resources to arrive at development cost and schedule estimates associated with various confidence levels.

[28] GAO, *NASA: Assessments of Selected Large-Scale Projects*, GAO-12-207SP (Washington, D.C.: March 1, 2012).

Until the program office conducts a schedule risk analysis on an integrated schedule that includes the entire scope of effort and addresses quality shortfalls of relevant component schedules, it will have less assurance of meeting the planned March 2017 launch date for JPSS-1.

NOAA Has Analyzed Alternatives for Addressing Gaps in Satellite Data, but Lacks a Comprehensive Contingency Plan

While NOAA has identified multiple ways to help mitigate expected gaps in polar satellite data, it has not yet developed and implemented a comprehensive contingency plan. In October 2012, NOAA established a plan to address the impact of potential gaps in polar afternoon satellite data and contracted for a technical assessment that generated additional alternatives for the agency to consider. However, NOAA's mitigation plan has shortfalls when compared to government and industry best practices. Moreover, NOAA intends to update its plan by fall 2013 by integrating alternatives generated from the contractor's technical assessment. Until NOAA establishes a comprehensive contingency plan that addresses key shortfalls, it may not be positioned to effectively mitigate anticipated gaps in polar satellite coverage.

NOAA Identified Multiple Ways to Mitigate Polar Satellite Data Gaps

Polar satellites are essential to NOAA's mission to understand and predict changes in climate, weather, oceans, and coasts. Satellite data gaps in the morning or afternoon polar orbits would lead to less accurate and timely weather forecasting; as a result, advanced warning of extreme events would be affected. In June 2012, we reported that while NOAA officials communicated publicly and often about the risk of a polar satellite data gap, the agency had not established plans to mitigate the gap.[29] We recommended that NOAA establish mitigation plans for pending satellite gaps in the afternoon orbit as well as potential gaps in the early morning and midmorning orbits and NOAA agreed with the report's recommendation.

In October 2012, NOAA established a mitigation plan to address the impact of potential gaps in polar afternoon satellite data. This plan identifies alternatives for mitigating the risk of a 14- to 18-month gap in the afternoon orbit beginning in March 2016, between the current polar satellite and the JPSS-1 satellite. Key alternatives include utilizing different satellites as data sources and improving data assimilation in models. The plan also lists technical, programmatic, and management

---

[29] GAO-12-604.

actions needed to implement these options. Table 9 provides an overview of NOAA's polar satellite gap mitigation plan.

Table 9: Summary of NOAA's Polar Satellite Gap Mitigation Plan

Key assumptions	Alternatives	Key actions	Implementation status
There would be a polar afternoon gap of 14 to 18 months between March 2016 and October 2017 (the date that JPSS-1 is to become operational) Mission critical data from S-NPP's ATMS, CrIS, and VIIRS instruments would be lost DOD and European satellites would continue providing data in the early morning and midmorning orbits, respectively	Use similar data from available sources, such as existing DOD, NOAA, and NASA polar satellites Improve NOAA data assimilation Rely on foreign data, including radio occultation data or future polar satellites from other nations such as Russia or China Use non-satellite sources, such as aircraft observations Use commercial solutions (although none were identified)	Technical: • Conduct data denial experiments eliminating afternoon polar-orbiting sounder data from forecast models • Calculate, obtain, and distribute the estimated end-of-life of all sounder and imagery satellite assets Programmatic: • Monitor and report monthly on the health of instruments on existing polar satellites • Augment NOAA research and development computing capability as soon as possible to run data impact experiments Management: • Commit to augmenting NOAA operational computing capability • Maintain international relationships that can result in partnerships for satellite data	Actions were not implemented or funded.

Source: GAO analysis of NOAA data.

However, NOAA did not implement the actions identified in its mitigation plan and decided to identify additional alternatives. In October 2012, at the direction of the Under Secretary of Commerce for Oceans and Atmosphere (who is also the NOAA Administrator), NOAA contracted for a detailed technical assessment of alternatives to mitigate the degradation of products caused by a gap in satellite data in the afternoon polar orbit. This assessment solicited input from experts within and outside of NOAA and resulted in the following alternatives:

- rely on DOD's DMSP satellite;

- expand the use of radio occultation data, including funding the ground segment for a follow-on United States/Taiwan radio occultation mission;

- use atmospheric motion vectors (observed wind data);

- utilize future geostationary advanced imagery data;

- expand the use of aircraft observations;

- expand the use of targeted observations for high-impact events;

- implement a 4-dimensional hybrid data assimilation system (by adding a time dimension) ;

- improve data assimilation of cloud-impacted radiances;

- implement blends of global models, such as European and Canadian models;

- accelerate global model research to operations;

- sustain the use of high-latitude direct readout imagery; and

- rely on China's future Feng Yun-3 satellite.

Moving forward, NOAA officials stated that they are currently considering the additional alternatives and that the agency intends to integrate a final set of alternatives into its existing mitigation plan by the fall of 2013.

NOAA Does Not Yet Have a Comprehensive Contingency Plan

Government and industry best practices call for the development of contingency plans to maintain an organization's essential functions in the case of an adverse event.[30] As a complement to risk mitigation, contingency planning includes strategies that attempt to reduce or control the impact of risks should they occur. These practices identified by, for example, the National Institute of Standards and Technology and the Software Engineering Institute, include key elements such as defining failure scenarios, identifying and selecting strategies to address failure scenarios, developing procedures and actions to implement the selected strategies, testing the plans, and involving affected stakeholders. These elements can be grouped into categories, including (1) identifying failure scenarios and impacts, (2) developing contingency plans, and (3) validating and implementing contingency plans (see table 10).

---

[30] See GAO, *Year 2000 Computing Crisis: Business Continuity and Contingency Planning*, GAO/AIMD-10.1.19 (Washington, D.C.: August 1998); National Institute of Standards and Technology, *Contingency Planning Guide for Federal Information Systems*, NIST 800-34 (May 2010); Software Engineering Institute, *CMMI® for Acquisition, Version 1.3* (Pittsburgh, Pa.: November 2010).

Table 10: Guidelines for Developing a Sound Contingency Plan

Category	Description
Identifying failure scenarios and impacts	This category includes activities such as defining failure scenarios; conducting impact analyses that show the impact of failure scenarios; defining minimum acceptable levels of outputs and recovery time objectives; and establishing resumption priorities.
Developing contingency plans	This category includes activities such as identifying alternative solutions to address failure scenarios; selecting contingency strategies from among alternatives based on costs, benefits, and impacts; defining actions, roles and responsibilities, triggers, and timelines for implementing contingency plans; developing "zero-day" procedures; ensuring that steps reflect priorities for resumption of products and recovery objectives; and obtaining review and approval of the contingency plan from designated officials.
Validating and implementing contingency plans	This category includes activities such as identifying steps for testing contingency plans and conducting training exercises; preparing for and executing tests; validating test results for consistency against minimum performance levels; executing applicable actions for implementation of contingency strategies; communicating and coordinating with stakeholders to ensure that contingency strategies remain optimal for reducing potential impacts; and updating and maintaining contingency plans as warranted.

Source: GAO analysis of guidance documents from the National Institute of Standards and Technology, Software Engineering Institute, and GAO.

By documenting its mitigation plan and conducting a study on additional alternatives, NOAA has taken positive steps towards establishing a contingency plan for handling the potential impact of satellite data gaps in the afternoon polar orbit. However, NOAA does not yet have a comprehensive contingency plan because it has not yet selected the strategies to be implemented, or established procedures and actions to implement the selected strategies. In addition, there are shortfalls in the agency's current plans as compared to government and industry best practices, such as not always identifying specific actions with defined roles and responsibilities, timelines, and triggers. Moreover, multiple steps remain in testing, validating, and implementing the contingency plan. The following table provides an assessment of the extent to which NOAA's mitigation plan met contingency planning practices in three general categories.

Table 11: Assessment of NOAA's Gap Mitigation Plan for its Polar Environmental Satellites

Contingency planning category	GAO assessment	Description
Identifying failure scenarios and impacts	Partially met	• The plan identifies key scenarios, such as an earlier than expected loss of data from the S-NPP satellite, a slip in the JPSS-1 launch date, a failure of JPSS-1 on launch, and a longer than expected calibration and validation period for JPSS-1.
		• The plan includes analyses of the impact to users from losing key weather products from ATMS, CrIS, and VIIRS. The plan also identifies minimum performance outputs for key weather data and reflects the top priorities identified in JPSS program requirements.
		• However, the plan does not address other scenarios, including the possibility of a loss of data from Department of Defense and European partner satellites in morning orbits or a partner mission in the afternoon orbit.
		• Further, the plan does not include recovery time objectives for key data products.
Developing contingency plans	Partially met	• The plan describes the impact of potential gaps in polar afternoon satellite data, identifies alternative strategies for mitigating the gap, and lists technical, programmatic, and management actions needed to implement gap mitigation strategies.
		• However, the plan has not yet been integrated with the other alternatives that were subsequently identified.
		• NOAA has not yet assessed its alternative strategies based on costs, benefits, and potential impacts.
		• The plan does not identify options for preventing gaps from occurring.
		• The plan does not identify opportunities for accelerating the calibration and validation phase—the time between launch and availability of operational products—on JPSS-1.
		• The plan does not identify specific actions for executing two of the five alternatives; identify roles and responsibilities for three alternatives; identify timelines for any of the alternatives; or identify triggers to signal when steps should be taken on any of the alternatives.
Validating and implementing contingency plans	Not met	• NOAA has not yet initiated efforts to validate or implement its gap mitigation plan.

Source: GAO analysis of NOAA data.

NOAA officials stated that the agency is continuing to work on refinements to its gap mitigation plan, and that they anticipate issuing an updated plan in fall 2013 that will reflect additional alternatives. While NOAA expects to update its plan, the agency does not yet have a schedule for adding key elements—such as specific actions, roles and responsibilities, timelines, and triggers—for each alternative. Until NOAA establishes a comprehensive contingency plan that integrates its strategies and addresses the elements identified above to improve its plans, it may not be sufficiently prepared to mitigate potential gaps in polar satellite coverage.

Conclusions

While NOAA has made noteworthy progress over the past year in utilizing S-NPP data in weather forecasts and developing instrument and spacecraft components of the JPSS-1 satellite, the agency is facing challenges in its efforts to ensure sustained satellite observations. Specifically, NOAA does not expect to validate key S-NPP products until September 2014—nearly 3 years after the satellite's launch. Also, the agency does not track the usage of its satellite products or obtain feedback on them, which limits the program's ability to ensure that satellite products are useful. Further, the program experienced scheduling problems on its ground systems, which led to a delay in planned system upgrades. Until NOAA establishes a way to track which agencies are using its products and to obtain feedback on those products, the program office may continue to experience delays in delivering actionable S-NPP data to users.

Almost 3 years after the JPSS program was established, it lacks a complete integrated master schedule. While program officials recently established a preliminary integrated master schedule, the schedule lacks proper linkage among dependent activities, which limits its ability to calculate dates and predict changes in the future. Further, the quality of component schedules varied for certain practices. These issues raise questions about the program's 70 percent joint cost and schedule confidence level in the JPSS-1 launch date. Until the program office develops a complete integrated schedule and addresses weaknesses in component schedules, it will lack the information needed to effectively monitor development progress and ensure the planned JPSS-1 launch date.

NOAA has taken steps to mitigate an anticipated gap in polar afternoon satellite data, but its efforts are incomplete. Specifically, the agency has not yet established a comprehensive contingency plan that identifies specific actions with defined roles and responsibilities, timelines, and triggers for contingency strategies. Moreover, the agency's recent assessment of a larger set of alternatives has not yet been integrated with its mitigation plans. As a result, the agency faces important decisions as to whether and how the various alternatives should be carried out. While NOAA plans to add alternatives to its mitigation plan by fall 2013, it does not yet have plans to add the other key components. Until NOAA establishes a comprehensive contingency plan that addresses these shortfalls, its plan for mitigating potential gaps in the polar orbit may not be effective in avoiding significant impacts to NOAA's weather mission.

Recommendations for Executive Action

Given the importance of having reliable schedules for managing JPSS satellite launch dates and the significance of polar-orbiting satellite data to weather forecasts, we recommend that the Secretary of Commerce direct the Administrator of NOAA to

- track the extent to which key groups of satellite data users are using S-NPP and JPSS products, and obtain feedback on these products;
- establish a complete JPSS program integrated master schedule that includes a logically linked sequence of activities;
- address the shortfalls in the ground system and spacecraft component schedules outlined in this report;
- after completing the integrated master schedule and addressing shortfalls in component schedules, update the joint cost and schedule confidence level for JPSS-1, if warranted and justified;
- establish a comprehensive contingency plan for potential satellite data gaps in the polar orbit that is consistent with contingency planning best practices identified in this report. The plan should include, for example, specific contingency actions with defined roles and responsibilities, timelines, and triggers; analysis of the impact of lost data from the morning orbits; and identification of opportunities to accelerate the calibration and validation phase of JPSS-1.

Agency Comments

We sought comments on a draft of our report from the Department of Commerce and NASA. We received written comments from Commerce transmitting NOAA's comments. NOAA concurred with all five of our recommendations and identified steps that it is taking to implement them. It also provided technical comments, which we have incorporated into our report, as appropriate. NOAA's comments are reprinted in appendix IV.

NASA did not provide comments on the report's findings or recommendations, but noted that it would provide any input it might have to NOAA for inclusion in NOAA's comments.

As agreed with your office, unless you publicly announce the contents of this report earlier, we plan no further distribution of it until 30 days from the date of this letter. We are sending copies of this report to interested congressional committees, the Secretary of Commerce, the Administrator of NASA, the Director of the Office of Management and Budget, and other interested parties. In addition, this report will be available on the GAO Web site at http://www.gao.gov.

If you or your staff have any questions on the matters discussed in this report, please contact me at (202) 512-9286 or at pownerd@gao.gov. Contact points for our Offices of Congressional Relations and Public Affairs may be found on the last page of this report. GAO staff who made major contributions to this report are listed in appendix V.

David A. Powner
Director, Information Technology
 Management Issues

Appendix I: Objectives, Scope, and Methodology

Our objectives were to (1) evaluate the National Oceanic and Atmospheric Administration's (NOAA) progress in meeting the Joint Polar Satellite System (JPSS) program's objectives of sustaining the continuity of NOAA's polar-orbiting satellite system through the Suomi National Polar-orbiting Partnership (S-NPP) and JPSS satellites, (2) evaluate the quality of the JPSS program schedule, and (3) assess NOAA's plans to address potential gaps in polar satellite data.

To evaluate NOAA's progress in meeting JPSS program objectives, we assessed (1) the status of activities supporting the operational S-NPP satellite, (2) progress on efforts to develop the JPSS-1 satellite, and (3) recent changes in JPSS program scope. A more detailed description of our activities in each of these areas follows.

- **S-NPP progress:** We reviewed monthly program reports to identify the status of key upgrades to the ground system supporting S-NPP and the efforts to transition operational control of the satellite to NOAA. In addition, we compared the program's current estimated completion dates for S-NPP products to original program estimates for when the products would be available for operational use. We compared program office information on the extent to which S-NPP products were being used to best practices in evaluating the use of completed products. We also interviewed program officials about algorithm maturity and the extent to which users are using S-NPP products.
- **JPSS-1 progress:** We analyzed plans and reports on system development efforts for the JPSS-1 satellite. Specifically, we reviewed the JPSS-1 mission preliminary design review package to assess completion of work on the instruments, spacecraft, and ground system as well as cost, schedule, and technical performance for the JPSS-1 satellite. We also examined JPSS program office monthly status reports on system development progress to identify variances and corrective actions being taken to address the most critical issues and risks to the program. We interviewed JPSS program officials to discuss system development status. We assessed the reliability of reported milestone dates for top-level milestones by examining multiple project status reports at different points in time for consistent reporting of dates or explanations of any changes and compared reported dates to source schedule data. We determined that the milestone data were sufficiently reliable for our reporting purposes.
- **Changes in JPSS program scope:** We compared the program's requirements as of September 2011 to the program's updated plans and requirements as of May 2013 to identify key changes and to

assess whether changes in capabilities have impacted program goals and objectives. We interviewed program officials about changes in the JPSS program's scope. We assessed the reliability of the program's estimated savings from program scope changes by comparing them to program documentation on prior and current cost estimates and found that the estimates were sufficient for our purposes.

To evaluate the quality of NOAA's program schedule, we used an exposure draft of GAO's Schedule Assessment Guide[1] to assess schedule management practices and characteristics of selected contractor schedules. We selected and analyzed three component contractor schedules—the ground system, the spacecraft, and the Visible/Infrared Imager/Radiometer Suite instrument—because these schedules represented the critical path for flight and the entire ground system development schedule that was either already or likely to be driving the JPSS-1 satellite launch date. We also analyzed schedule metrics as a part of that analysis to highlight potential areas of strengths and weakness in, among other things, schedule logic, use of resources, task duration, float, and task completion. In order to assess each schedule against the ten best practices, we traced and verified underlying support and determined whether the program office or contractor provided a small portion, about half, a large portion, or complete evidence that satisfied the criterion and assigned a score depicting that the practices were met, minimally met, partially met, substantially met, or fully met. By examining the schedules against our guidance, we conducted a reliability assessment on each of the schedules and incorporated our findings on reliability limitations in the analysis of each component schedule. We reviewed documentation on a schedule risk assessment the JPSS program office conducted on JPSS-1 flight project schedules to identify assumptions and results of its analysis and to assess the reliability of the reported JPSS joint cost and schedule confidence level. We interviewed government and contractor officials to discuss reasons for observed shortfalls in schedule management practices. We determined that the schedules were sufficiently reliable for our reporting purposes and our report notes the instances where reliability concerns affect the quality of the schedules as well as the program's schedule risk assessment.

---

[1] GAO Schedule Assessment Guide: Best Practices for Project Schedules, GAO-12-120G (exposure draft) (Washington, D.C.: May 30, 2012).

To assess plans to address potential gaps in polar satellite data, we
reviewed NOAA's October 2012 polar satellite gap mitigation plan and a
subsequent technical assessment as well as NOAA's plans for
implementing recommendations from the assessment. We compared
elements of the plan and assessment against best practices developed
from leading government and industry sources such as the National
Institute of Standards and Technology, the Software Engineering
Institute's Capability Maturity Model® Integration, and our prior report.
Based on that analysis, we identified shortfalls in NOAA's current plans
as well as key remaining activities for the agency to accomplish. We
interviewed NOAA headquarters staff and JPSS program officials about
the technical assessment and their plans.

We performed our work at NASA and NOAA offices in the Washington,
D.C. area. We conducted this performance audit from October 2012
through September 2013 in accordance with generally accepted
government auditing standards. Those standards require that we plan
and perform the audit to obtain sufficient, appropriate evidence to provide
a reasonable basis for our findings and conclusions based on our audit
objectives. We believe that the evidence obtained provides a reasonable
basis for our findings and conclusions based on our audit objectives.

Appendix II: NOAA Plans to Transfer Selected JPSS Program Components to the Polar Free Flyer Program

In order to reduce Joint Polar Satellite System (JPSS) program costs and increase the program's focus on its weather mission, the National Oceanic and Atmospheric Administration (NOAA) plans to transfer key program components to a separate program, called the Polar Free Flyer program. After establishing JPSS in 2010, NOAA committed to developing three units of the Total and Spectral Solar Irradiance Sensor (TSIS) and to finding a spacecraft and launch accommodation for three instruments that would not be on the JPSS satellite: TSIS, the Advanced Data Collection System (A-DCS), and the Search and Rescue Satellite-Aided Tracking (SARSAT) system. As of June 2012, the JPSS program planned to launch two stand-alone satellites (called free flyers) to accommodate two suites of these instruments. However, NOAA recently made several decisions that affect these commitments, and expects to finalize these plans by the end of September 2013:

- NOAA plans to transfer responsibility for developing TSIS and accommodating the launch of the three instruments out of the JPSS program and into a newly established Polar Free Flyer program. According to JPSS program officials, a transition plan for the new program is under review and selected staff positions have been filled.
- The Polar Free Flyer program will deliver a single free flyer mission instead of the two missions planned under the JPSS program.
- NOAA will transfer the responsibility for developing the second TSIS instrument to the National Aeronautics and Space Administration (NASA), rely on an Air Force Global Positioning System mission to continue SARSAT coverage, and find a launch vehicle to accommodate an additional A-DCS instrument.
- NOAA plans to use the JPSS ground system to support the Polar Free Flyer Program.

The JPSS program plans to award a contract in fiscal year 2014 for a spacecraft that is to accommodate the TSIS, A-DCS, and SARSAT instruments. The three instruments are in development and testing, and are expected to be delivered to the satellite by 2015. The planned launch readiness date for the free-flyer mission was originally July 2016, but that date may change pending the outcome of the spacecraft contract award. Also, the program is looking to share a launch vehicle with some other mission to reduce launch costs. However, the program office is not aware of any ride-sharing opportunities that could accommodate the mission's planned launch readiness date.

Appendix III: Assessment of JPSS Component Schedules Implementation of Best Practices in Scheduling

The following tables identify detailed assessments of the extent to which three component schedules supporting the JPSS-1 schedule met the ten best practices and four characteristics of a high-quality, reliable schedule. Table 12 provides an assessment of the ground system contractor's schedule, which integrates activities from seven components of the ground system; table 13 provides an assessment of the spacecraft contractor's detailed schedule; and table 14 provides an assessment of the VIIRS contractor's detailed schedule.

The following information describes the key that we used in tables 12 through 14 to convey the results of our assessment of the schedules' consistency with an exposure draft of GAO best practices for schedule management.[1]

● Met: The program office or contractor provided complete evidence that satisfies the entire criterion.

◕ Substantially met: The program office or contractor provided evidence that satisfies a large portion of the criterion.

◑ Partially met: The program office or contractor provided evidence that satisfies about half of the criterion.

◔ Minimally met: The program office or contractor provided evidence that satisfies a small portion of the criterion.

○ Not met: The program office or contractor provided no evidence that satisfies any of the criterion.

Table 12: Detailed Assessment of Ground System Schedule Quality

Schedule characteristic or best practice	GAO assessment	Examples of strengths and weaknesses
Comprehensive		
Capturing all activities	◕	The schedule largely reflects the statement of work. However, the schedule only partially reflects the work breakdown structure and includes 40 activities that are marked as both summary activities and milestones.
Assigning resources to all activities	◕	The contractor has established a clear process for integrating information between the schedule and the resource management software. However, resource leveling has been performed outside of the schedule, which limits the effectiveness of the process.
Establishing the duration of all activities	◕	According to the contractor, durations were estimated by the people responsible for the activities based on work to be done. Additionally, calendars were used to specify valid working times for all activities. However, over 35 percent of the activities in the schedule were of long duration, and only half of these were justified in schedule documentation.

---

[1] *GAO Schedule Assessment Guide: Best Practices for Project Schedules*, GAO-12-120G (exposure draft) (Washington, D.C.: May 30, 2012).

Schedule characteristic or best practice	GAO assessment	Examples of strengths and weaknesses
Well-constructed		
Sequencing all activities	◑	A majority of the activities in the schedule had dependencies, and the schedule's relationships were largely finish-to-start. However, program officials did not justify in schedule documentation the small number of activities with missing dependencies, date constraints, and lags.
Confirming that the critical path is valid	◔	The critical path and driving path are not fully valid because they are not free of long activities, constraints, and lags. Moreover, considering the schedule as a whole, the schedule software may not be calculating the true critical path of the project because the use of more than 800 constraints. These may result in float values that present an unrealistic view of the critical path.
Ensuring reasonable total float	◑	According to contractor officials, float values have been assessed as part of regularly scheduled health checks and they have determined that for certain cases float values are necessarily high. However, not all float values calculated by the schedule are reasonable and many values do not accurately reflect true schedule flexibility. Additionally, the JPSS program office did not provide a documented assessment of total float values that appear to be excessive to show that the team agrees with the logic and that the float is consistent with the plan.
Credible		
Verifying that the schedule can be traced horizontally and vertically	◑	The schedule is vertically traceable in all but one of the milestones that we reviewed, meaning that it allows activity owners to trace activities to higher-level milestones with intermediate and summary schedules. However, the schedule is not fully horizontally traceable—that is, although the schedule includes giver/receiver milestones that are defined in the schedule documentation, the schedule was not always affected by activities whose durations were extended by hundreds of days.
Conducting a schedule risk analysis	◔	The contractor conducted a schedule risk analysis with a schedule network that partially meets the characteristics associated with a good schedule network, as well three point duration estimates that were captured from control account managers. However, the analysis was conducted for select near-term milestones—not to the readiness of the ground system for the launch of JPSS-1. Additionally, the analysis did not include risks most likely to delay the project, the paths or activities that are most likely to delay the project, and the activities that most often ended up on the critical path.
Controlled		
Updating the schedule using actual progress and logic	◕	Responsibility for changing the schedule has been assigned to someone who has the proper training and experience in critical path method scheduling and the schedule is free of clearly erroneous progress information. However, although the contractor provides a monthly program management briefing that addresses the status of external giver/receiver activities, it does not address the status of key milestone dates, changes in network logic, or critical paths.
Maintaining a baseline schedule	◕	A baseline schedule exists and is compared to the current schedule to track variances from the plan. According to contractor officials, a formal change control process is used to make changes to the baseline. However, the contractor's rolling wave reports do not satisfy all elements of a baseline schedule document. A baseline schedule document is a single document that describes, among other things, the organization of the IMS; the logic of the network; the basic approach to managing resources; the schedule's unique features; and justification for lags, date constraints, and long activity durations.

Source: GAO analysis of JPSS program office and contractor schedule data.

Table 13: Detailed Assessment of Spacecraft Schedule Quality

Schedule characteristic or best practice	GAO assessment	Examples of strengths and weaknesses
Comprehensive		
Capturing all activities	◐	The schedule reflects the work necessary to build the spacecraft, and schedule activities are mapped to the contract data requirements list and contractor work breakdown structure numbers. The schedule contains a low level of detail, which reflects the contractor's role as integrator for multiple vendors in a fixed-price environment. However, with a nearly 1:1 ratio of detail activities to milestones, the schedule would benefit from increased detail into work activities.
Assigning resources to all activities	◑	The contractor has established a clear process for integrating information between the schedule and the resource management software. However, resource leveling has been performed outside of the schedule, which limits the effectiveness of the process.
Establishing the duration of all activities	◐	The contractor has experience in developing spacecraft similar to JPSS-1, including S-NPP. Contractor officials stated that they obtained duration estimates for activities from engineers that were responsible for them while other engineers conducted peer reviews on those estimates. However, durations in general appear too long to facilitate objective measurement of accomplished effort. Even accounting for procurement-related activities and level-of-effort type recurring meeting activities, one-third of all remaining activities are longer than 2 business months.
Well-constructed		
Sequencing all activities	◐	The schedule was partially logically sequenced. Approximately 20 percent of all remaining activities and milestones were missing predecessor links, successor links or both. Officials stated that many of these activities were related to contract data requirements list deliveries and internal or external handoffs (called givers/receivers). We found other areas of questionable sequencing logic. For instance, there are about 10 percent of remaining activities in the schedule that have lags and leads, including some instances of leads with start-to-finish logic—a particularly abnormal logical relationship. We also found date constraints pervasive throughout the schedule: 140 activities have soft constraints and 17 have hard constraints. Hard constraints are useful for calculating the amount of float available in the schedule and, therefore, the realism of the required project finish date and available resources during schedule development. However, they may be abused if they force activities to occur on specific dates that are determined off-line without much regard for the realism of the assumptions necessary to achieve them.
Confirming that the critical path is valid	◐	The schedule defines activities with zero total float as critical. However, partly because of logic issues, the critical path as calculated by the scheduling software was convoluted and most likely unreliable. The path includes lags, leads, long-duration activities, and activities with hard constraints, which by definition will appear as critical. Officials stated they agreed that software-calculated critical paths cannot be relied upon in a complex schedule, and said they report the longest (or driving path) to management. Ideally, the critical path and the longest path should be the same, but our analysis found the longest path to be somewhat different than the default critical path; it does not include several activities that appeared on the critical path because of their date constraints. In addition, the longest path also includes several near-term, nonprocurement-related activities with long durations, spanning between 84 and 365 days.

Schedule characteristic or best practice	GAO assessment	Examples of strengths and weaknesses
Ensuring reasonable total float	◑	Officials stated that the total float values calculated by the schedule accurately reflect true schedule flexibility. However, we found that the schedule appears overly flexible due to high amounts of total float. 70 percent of remaining activities and milestones have greater than 30 days (about 5 business weeks) of total float. This includes 67 activities (8 percent of remaining) with over 1,000 days of float, meaning these activities can slip more than 3.5 business years before impacting the planned finish date of the project. Without documented justification for high float values in the schedule, it is not clear which are explained by milestones without successors, which are due to schedule maintenance, and which are due to incomplete logic.
Credible		
Verifying that the schedule can be traced horizontally and vertically	◑	The schedule is vertically traceable, with dates in the detail schedule mapping to higher-level management briefing charts. The schedule is generally horizontally traceable. The schedule clearly identifies givers and receivers and negative total float calculations respond appropriately when significant delays are introduced into the network. However, negative float is calculated because key milestones are constrained. While the negative float may be an accurate assessment of potential delay, management may not be aware of potential delays when constrained dates are reported in summary-level schedules.
Conducting a schedule risk analysis	◑	Officials stated that they follow an internal process to perform schedule risk analyses on the schedule. Officials also stated that three-point durations are applied to activities, correlation is accounted for, and a Monte Carlo analysis is run on the schedule to derive probabilities for forecasted dates. Although the contractor has no contractual requirement to share schedule risk analysis results with the JPSS program office, it provided a summary of its risk assessment report and instructions. However, this summary information did not include supporting details such as risk data inputs and data normalization techniques and the contractor did not incorporate correlation or perform the schedule risk analysis on a logically sound (well-constructed) schedule.
Controlled		
Updating the schedule using actual progress and logic	◕	Schedule progress is updated monthly and the schedule is delivered to the JPSS program office in accordance with contractual requirements. While a formal schedule narrative does not accompany the schedule delivery to the government, much of the narrative information—such as the status of key milestones and handoffs, explanations for changes in key dates, and an overview of critical and near-critical paths—is conveyed in monthly management meetings. However, 26 activities had start or finish dates in the past. Of these, 12 activities could be explained by obsolete scope of work. We also found 12 out-of-sequence activities, representing 13 percent of in-progress activities.
Maintaining a baseline schedule	◑	Contractor officials stated that they maintain schedule baseline information in the default baseline fields in the schedule and we found that baseline dates were set in the schedule. However, a schedule baseline document was not created for the schedule baseline. We found 104 activities in the schedule without baseline dates, 72 of which are complete or are planned to start by 2014. The majority of start variances appear reasonable, but we did find start variances ranging from -221 days (221 days ahead of schedule) to 237 days (237 days delayed). Despite the significant variances noted, it is commendable that the schedule includes baseline information that allows for analysis and monitoring of dates' variances.

Source: GAO analysis of JPSS program office and contractor schedule data.

Table 14: Detailed Assessment of VIIRS Schedule Quality

Schedule characteristic or best practice	GAO assessment	Examples of strengths and weaknesses
Comprehensive		
Capturing all activities	◑	The schedule largely reflects the work breakdown structure and statement of work. However, the schedule does not reflect work to be performed by a subcontractor and includes 10 activities that are marked as both summary activities and milestones.
Assigning resources to all activities	◑	The contractor has established a clear process for integrating information between the schedule and the resource management software. However, resource leveling has been performed outside of the schedule, which limits the effectiveness of the process.
Establishing the duration of all activities	●	According to the contractor, durations were estimated by the people responsible for the activities based on work to be done, realistic assumptions about available resources, productivity, normal interferences and distractions, and reliance on others. Further, the contractor justified in its schedule documentation virtually all activities with durations longer than 44 days.
Well-constructed		
Sequencing all activities	◑	All but one activity in the schedule has at least one predecessor and one successor, and that activity was justified in the schedule documentation. Additionally, every schedule date constraint was justified in schedule documentation. However, the schedule has a very small number of activities with dangling logic. Further, although explanations were provided for most of the small number of lags, the explanations did not justify their use.
Confirming that the critical path is valid	◑	Program office and contractor officials use the driving path to manage the program, which is preferred because it represents the activities that are driving the sequence of start dates directly affecting the estimated finish date. However, the driving path and the critical path to key milestones should be the same, and they are not. Also, the critical path is not valid because it contains level of effort activities.
Ensuring reasonable total float	◑	The program office has defined reasonable float values, and the values associated with the schedule largely fit that definition. For those float values that were not reasonable, the program office provided a documented assessment of those values to show that the team agrees with the logic and that the float is consistent with the plan. However, the schedule has a small number of activities that have unrealistic float values.
Credible		
Verifying that the schedule can be traced horizontally and vertically	◑	The schedule is largely horizontally traceable. In particular, the schedule is affected by activities whose durations are extended by hundreds of days, and it includes giver/receiver milestones that represent handoffs between contractor integrated project teams. However, the schedule does not include all givers/receivers between the contractor and the program office. Additionally, the schedule is vertically traceable. Specifically, it allows activity owners to trace activities to higher-level milestones with intermediate and summary schedules.
Conducting a schedule risk analysis	◔	A schedule risk analysis was conducted with a good schedule network, and three point duration estimates that were captured from subject matter experts. However, the duration estimates did not reflect risks from the project's risk register and the analysis was focused on only the deterministic critical path and near-critical path.

Schedule characteristic or best practice	GAO assessment	Examples of strengths and weaknesses
Controlled		
Updating the schedule using actual progress and logic	●	Responsibility for changing or updating the schedule has been assigned to someone who has the proper training and experience in critical path method scheduling. Additionally, the schedule is free of clearly erroneous progress information. Further, the contractor provides a schedule narrative accompanying each status update, which describes the status of key milestone dates (including the program finish date); explanations for changes in key dates; and a description of the critical paths.
Maintaining a baseline schedule	◑	A baseline schedule exists and is compared to the current schedule to track variances. However, the contractor did not have a baseline schedule document. A baseline schedule document is a single document that describes, among other things, the organization of the IMS; the logic of the network; the basic approach to managing resources; the schedule's unique features; and justification for lags, date constraints, and long activity durations.

Source: GAO analysis of JPSS program office and contractor schedule data.

Appendix IV: Comments from the Department of Commerce

THE DEPUTY SECRETARY OF COMMERCE
Washington, D.C. 20230

August 26, 2013

Mr. David A. Powner
Director
Information Technology Management Issues
U.S. Government Accountability Office
441 G Street NW
Washington, DC 20548

Dear Mr. Powner:

Thank you for the opportunity to review and comment on the Government Accountability Office (GAO) draft report entitled "Polar Weather Satellites: NOAA Identified Ways to Mitigate Data Gaps, but Contingency Plans and Schedules Require Further Attention" (GAO-13-676). On behalf of the Department of Commerce, I have enclosed the National Oceanic and Atmospheric Administration's programmatic comments to the draft report. At your request, we are conducting a sensitivity review and will notify you of the results when our review is complete.

If you have any questions, please contact me or Margaret Cummisky, Assistant Secretary for Legislative and Intergovernmental Affairs at (202) 482-3663.

Sincerely,

Patrick Gallagher
Acting Deputy Secretary of Commerce

Enclosure

Department of Commerce
National Oceanic and Atmospheric Administration Response to
GAO Draft Report "Polar Weather Satellites - NOAA Identified
Ways to Mitigate Data Gaps, but Contingency Plans
and Schedules Require Further Attention"
(GAO-13-676)

General Comments

The Department of Commerce's National Oceanic and Atmospheric Administration (NOAA) appreciates the opportunity to review the Government Accountability Office (GAO) draft report on Polar Weather Satellites. The draft report on Polar Weather Satellites product development, program schedule, and potential gaps does a fair job of assessing the state of the program. Given the history and changes in the polar-orbiting operational environment satellite programs over the past decade, NOAA recommends the following changes and updates to the report to ensure that the information presented is complete, up-to-date, and reflects current plans.

NOAA Response to GAO Recommendations

The draft GAO report states "Given the importance of having reliable schedules for managing JPSS satellite launch dates and the significance of polar-orbiting satellite data to weather forecasts, we recommend the Secretary of Commerce direct the Administrator of NOAA to"—

Recommendation 1: "Track the extent to which groups of satellite data users are using S-NPP and JPSS products and obtain feedback on these products."

NOAA Response: NOAA agrees with this recommendation. NOAA is already tracking the use of S-NPP products by key user groups such as the NWS/NCEP. For example, NOAA uses the Joint Center for Satellite Data Assimilation (JCSDA) to assess the impacts of new data sources on Numerical Weather Predication. NOAA also utilizes existing partner forums to receive feedback from non-NOAA users such as EUMETSAT and DoD. NOAA will expand its tracking to include all S-NPP and JPSS products used by NOAA programs and partner organizations.

Recommendation 2: "establish a complete JPSS program integrated master schedule that includes a logically linked sequence of activities;"

NOAA Response: NOAA agrees with this recommendation. NOAA could not complete two parts of the Integrated Master Schedule (IMS) by the time of the System Definition Review (SDR) due to contracting efforts underway but not completed. However, risk was mitigated by including the preliminary schedules and having an acceptable plan for closure. The IMS will be completed by January 2014 when contractual modifications required to support the ground segment have been finalized. Nevertheless, the JPSS program has made tremendous progress on maturing its schedule and has confidence in it. This is supported by independent review results of the SDR and the confirmation of the JPSS performance baseline (indicated by completing the Key Decision Point-I) by the Acting Deputy Secretary of Commerce.

Recommendation 3: "address the shortfalls in the ground system and spacecraft component schedules outlined in this report;"

NOAA Response: NOAA agrees with this recommendation. NOAA will address this recommendation by updating the ground system and spacecraft component schedules based on the recent completion of its SRR and KDP-1 reviews. In addition, we will continue to monitor and analyze these schedules on a monthly basis.

Recommendation 4: "after completing the integrated master schedule and addressing shortfalls in component schedules, update the joint cost and schedule confidence level for JPSS-1, if warranted and justified;"

NOAA Response: NOAA agrees with this recommendation. NOAA will update the JPSS-1 joint cost and schedule confidence levels after completing the IMS, if warranted and justified.

Recommendation 5: "establish a comprehensive contingency plan for potential satellite data gaps in the polar orbit that is consistent with the contingency planning best practices identified in this report. The plan should include, for example, specific contingency actions with defined roles and responsibilities, timelines, and triggers; analysis of the impact of lost data from the morning orbits, and identification of opportunities to accelerate the calibration and validation phases of JPSS-1."

NOAA Response: NOAA agrees with this recommendation. NOAA acknowledges the need to develop a more comprehensive contingency plan for polar-orbiting satellite data gaps, including gaps in the early and mid-morning orbits. NOAA plans to update the current Gap Mitigation Plan in the fall of 2013 and continue to update the plan approximately every 6 months. This update will include a first iteration addressing items identified in the recommendation.

Contingency actions are of two categories: (1) those which may be taken to decrease the probability of a gap occurring once a triggering event occurs (or decreasing the duration of a gap that occurs), and (2) those mitigating the impact of a gap once a triggering event occurs. It should be noted that for applications such as numerical weather prediction modeling, the methods of mitigating the impact of a gap include improving the NWP models themselves, improving the data assimilation system to optimize the impact of the data used in the model, and developing means of increasing the fraction of available data assimilated, for example using satellite data that are affected by clouds and precipitation. These methods would be the same no matter which gap or combination of gaps might occur—early, mid-morning, or afternoon. Hence the usefulness of assessing the impact of gaps in each orbit is limited. Moreover, efforts to quantify each gap impact will compete for resources with efforts that would limit the impact of any of the potential gaps. Therefore, our plan must be judicious in applying resources.

Appendix V: GAO Contact and Staff Acknowledgments

GAO Contact	David A. Powner (202) 512-9286 or pownerd@gao.gov.
Staff Acknowledgments	In addition to the contact named above, Colleen Phillips (Assistant Director), Paula Moore (Assistant Director), Shaun Byrnes, Juaná Collymore, Lynn Espedido, Kate Feild, Nancy Glover, Franklin Jackson, Kaelin Kuhn, Jason Lee, Joshua Leiling, and Maria Stattel made key contributions to this report.

GAO's Mission	The Government Accountability Office, the audit, evaluation, and investigative arm of Congress, exists to support Congress in meeting its constitutional responsibilities and to help improve the performance and accountability of the federal government for the American people. GAO examines the use of public funds; evaluates federal programs and policies; and provides analyses, recommendations, and other assistance to help Congress make informed oversight, policy, and funding decisions. GAO's commitment to good government is reflected in its core values of accountability, integrity, and reliability.
Obtaining Copies of GAO Reports and Testimony	The fastest and easiest way to obtain copies of GAO documents at no cost is through GAO's website (http://www.gao.gov). Each weekday afternoon, GAO posts on its website newly released reports, testimony, and correspondence. To have GAO e-mail you a list of newly posted products, go to http://www.gao.gov and select "E-mail Updates."
Order by Phone	The price of each GAO publication reflects GAO's actual cost of production and distribution and depends on the number of pages in the publication and whether the publication is printed in color or black and white. Pricing and ordering information is posted on GAO's website, http://www.gao.gov/ordering.htm. Place orders by calling (202) 512-6000, toll free (866) 801-7077, or TDD (202) 512-2537. Orders may be paid for using American Express, Discover Card, MasterCard, Visa, check, or money order. Call for additional information.
Connect with GAO	Connect with GAO on Facebook, Flickr, Twitter, and YouTube. Subscribe to our RSS Feeds or E-mail Updates. Listen to our Podcasts. Visit GAO on the web at www.gao.gov.
To Report Fraud, Waste, and Abuse in Federal Programs	Contact: Website: http://www.gao.gov/fraudnet/fraudnet.htm E-mail: fraudnet@gao.gov Automated answering system: (800) 424-5454 or (202) 512-7470
Congressional Relations	Katherine Siggerud, Managing Director, siggerudk@gao.gov, (202) 512-4400, U.S. Government Accountability Office, 441 G Street NW, Room 7125, Washington, DC 20548
Public Affairs	Chuck Young, Managing Director, youngc1@gao.gov, (202) 512-4800 U.S. Government Accountability Office, 441 G Street NW, Room 7149 Washington, DC 20548

Please Print on Recycled Paper.